D0929911

THE

PHOENIX LIBRARY

*

TWENTIETH CENTURY
POETRY

*A list
of other titles in the Phoenix Library
will be found at the end
of this book*

TWENTIETH CENTURY POETRY

AN ANTHOLOGY CHOSEN

By

HAROLD MONRO

CHATTO AND WINDUS

LONDON
Republished 1977
SCHOLARLY PRESS, INC.
19722 E. Nine Mile Rd., St. Clair Shores, Michigan 48080

First issued in the Phoenix Library
First publication 1929
Reprinted 1930 (twice), 1931

Library of Congress Cataloging in Publication Data

Monro, Harold, 1879–1931, comp.
   Twentieth century poetry; an anthology.

   Reprint of the 1930 ed. published by Chatto and
Windus, London, in series: The Phoenix library.
   1. English poetry—20th century. I. Title.
II. Series: The Phoenix library.
PRJ.225.M57 1974   821'.9'1208   74-3111
ISBN 0-403-03062-5

INTRODUCTION

It is claimed for this anthology :

I   That it has not been compiled (according to frequent custom) from the multitudinous others of the past twenty years.

II   That it is the product of a wide and diligent investigation of nearly all the books published in this century, and of most of those published toward the end of the last, so as to ensure that our intrinsic period might be fully portrayed.

III   That about 600 volumes have been re-read or newly read, to refresh the memory, and to make a foundation for the structure of the book.

The name of the book should not be accepted too literally. Its intention is to cover the whole of our own period. What then is *our* Period ? Chronological Pedantry would naturally confine it within certain decades.

II

Emerson wrote : " The experience of each age requires a new confession, and the world seems always waiting for its poet." But Cowley wrote : " A war-like, various and tragical age is best to write of, but worst to write in." And J. M. Synge : " Before verse can become human again it must become brutal." All three quotations can be applied to our own period ; and I have tried to make this " war-like and tragical age " speak as clearly and authentically as it can through the mouth of its own poetry.

Certain chronological boundaries were necessary, though as arbitrary as possible. As the selection proceeded, it gradually became a general rule, with the older poets, to include those only whose *Collected Works* had been published within the Century. Automatically excluded are such poets

7

as Ernest Dowson and Lionel Johnson, authentic children of the Eighteen-Nineties.

John Davidson, an intermittent indifferent member of The Rhymer's Club, might be thought to belong to the last century (though he drowned himself in 1909). But he belongs rather to our own, and the two poems by which he is represented are so little known that I could not resist them. On the same lines, it might be argued that the magnificent Gerard Manley Hopkins should have no room. But Chronology may now be dropped, he belonging temperamentally and technically to the Twentieth Century, not to the Nineteenth.

Among other inclusions are four poets of American origin, one of whom has now become a British subject. There is no need for controversy on the point. This anthology is not Anglo-American. America now has a poetry of its own. But these three or four are included, not chiefly because their works were first published in England (for also were those of other Americans), but because their influences or their reputations here have been such as to render them essential to the scheme of the book.

" War Poems " interlock with and overlap all others right through, for the young authors who suddenly (as it were) burst out in flame through a fierce indignation against the war are like a central pivot to the period, and were more than partly instrumental in the fresh impulse given, thus, indirectly, to our English poetry.

Lastly, as regards my own poems. It has been the policy of some editors (who have been also poets) to exclude themselves altogether, of others to select themselves to the extent of one item ; and again of others unreluctantly to lavish their gifts. I can only plead that I handed all my material to an impartial judge, who, having examined the whole manuscript of the anthology, gave, with regard to myself, the verdict of an umpire, I having previously agreed not to dispute it.

8

So much for inclusions. I would rather have asked its readers to enjoy this anthology if they could, without any Introduction or Apology. But it gradually became evident that explanations must be offered. Why, for instance, are some of the more famous poets of the moment so thinly represented? The reply (controversial immediately!) is: That they were read again, and . . .

An examination of literary history reveals that in nearly every decade a poet arises who is hailed as a pride and a wonder by a worthy public without any clear discrimination. Thus, once, Bloomfield, or Montgomery, or Alexander Smith; (thus: Tupper); thus too, Sir Lewis Morris, and Sir Edwin Arnold; then, even the dramatic poet, Stephen Phillips, who has now faded,—but in this century nobody shall be named (unless, our best-seller, John Oxenham). So, to each decade its poet: Centuries think in different terms.

I have tried to find, and rejoiced when I could find, some excellent qualities in poets in whom I did not expect them. The third, or thereabout, of a century that we are now leaving behind us, when truly examined, becomes portentously prolific. Is it a great big period, or a minutely small? Reply who can! Somebody with whom I was talking cried: "They are all only poetical persons—*not* poets. Who will be reading them a century hence?" To which I answered: "There are so many of them that, a century hence, they may appear a kind of Composite Poet; there may be 500 excellent poems proceeding from 100 poets mostly not so very great, but well worth remembering a century hence."

If so, how many, I wonder, of those 500 poems, figure in the following anthology?

Surely, however, the period of Hardy and Bridges, leading on to Flecker and Brooke, may be called *Great*, if one must use the word. The "Georgian" Anthologies (in which the last two figured) represented another definite period in the public mind, which however was unduly shortened, for the chief part, by an excessive production of other similar anthologies, culminating in a natural fatigue. Mr. A. E.

Housman may be called the spiritual father of the movement, as Mr. E. Marsh was its temporal patron.

To-day we have each our *Waste Land*, and the strong influence of Mr. T. S. Eliot, and a few other poets, chiefly unacknowledged in Georgian circles, is more indicative of future tendencies than any other recognizable Signpost. I should say that just as A. E. Housman and Rupert Brooke were very powerful influences up to 1920, so T. S. Eliot will be up to 1940. The former, however, carved jewels, while the latter rough-models out of block granite.

Though I claim not to be a Chronological Pedant, nevertheless a mild chronological tendency has been maintained in the following pages. Thus, Bridges, Hardy, Flecker, Brooke, Yeats, Blunt, are represented almost entirely in the first half ; whereas the later part consists rather of Eliot, Aldington, Ezra Pound, the writers of very short lyrics, the Sitwells, and Peter Quennell. Nevertheless a dovetail will be clear, certain tendencies being allowed to appear too early and others apparently to persist just a little too late for the sake of exemplifying the complex development of the whole period. In certain cases the omission of poems that it was desired to include has been due to circumstances beyond editorial control.

Another tendency has been to give preference to the shorter, and, if possible, the lyrical poetry, and generally, in respect of the temperament or character of any given poet, to represent him rather by the more typical than by the more famous of his works. Thus, after anxious deliberation, many of the Show-Poems of other anthologies have been omitted. Such are The Listeners, Cargoes, Innisfree, The Dead, Leisure, Music Comes, The Oxen, The Bells of Heaven, The Shepherdess, To a Bull Dog, Everyone Sang.

" But," it may be asked, " if these have been so loudly acclaimed, must they not be among the best poems of their respective authors ? " I cannot answer. I only know that it has become so much a habit to reprint and to quote them, that for fear of making of any of them an *Excelsior* or a *Casabianca*, it seemed necessary to exclude.

10

Our long poems, from Darwin to Wells, have been written chiefly in prose, though we must not forget *The Dynasts* and *The Dawn in Britain,* which future generations will read increasingly. The period is one of short poems, and of impatient readers.

The habit of sharp contrast and of anticlimax is much practised. We find it in John Masefield, as in T. S. Eliot, each in his own manner, and carried to absurdity by inferior imitators. Nature Poems remain very prominent. It is difficult and tedious to wade, or paddle, through some of the packed and stiff volumes. The more beautiful usually concern birds. The obtrusive starling has more than once been chased away, yet even so he nearly managed to predominate over the numerous other birds in the Collection.

Some shorter poems of the period are so intelligent, graphic and witty that it is very hard to distinguish them from super-journalism, or to hazard how posterity will receive and judge of them.

A discussion of what is known as *free verse* must not here be broached. The matter is controversial and subject to much misunderstanding. The influence, however, will be clear in the following pages and the tendency definite. I will refer the reader to Mr. T. S. Eliot's Introduction to the Poems of Ezra Pound.

Lastly, Reader, please do not base your judgment too dogmatically upon inclusions and exclusions. I have thought of the book in terms of a Building. You are left to judge its main proportions. Above all, may it delight you !

ACKNOWLEDGEMENTS

GRATEFUL thanks are due to the following for their kind permission to reprint the copyright poems included in these pages :—The Author and George Allen & Unwin Ltd. (Richard Aldington) ; the Authors and Ernest Benn Ltd. (Richard Church, Camilla Doyle) ; Basil Blackwell (Edith Sitwell) ; Wm. Blackwood & Sons Ltd. (Alfred Noyes, ' Seagulls on the Serpentine ' from ' Ballads and Poems ') ; Burns Oates & Washbourne (1929) Ltd. (Alice Meynell) ; Jonathan Cape Ltd. (Samuel Butler, W. H. Davies) ; the Authors and Chatto & Windus (Harold Monro, Robert Nichols, Wilfred Owen, Peter Quennell, W. J. Turner, Sylvia Townsend Warner) ; the Author and W. Collins Sons & Co. Ltd. (Edward Shanks) ; the Authors and Constable & Co. Ltd. (Gordon Bottomley, ' Babel ' from ' Poems of Thirty Years ', Walter de la Mare, ' Who ? ', and ' Drugged ' from ' The Veil and Other Poems ', ' The Linnet ' and ' The Song of the Mad Prince ' from Poems 1901 to 1918 (2 vols.)) ; the Authors and Gerald Duckworth & Co. Ltd. (Edith Sitwell, Osbert Sitwell, Sacheverell Sitwell) ; the Authors and Faber & Faber Ltd. (T. S. Eliot, Herbert Read) ; William Heine-mann Ltd. (Isaac Rosenberg) ; The Hogarth Press (Edwin Muir) ; the Author and The Incorporated Society of Authors, Playwrights and Composers (John Masefield, ' The Yarn of the Loch Achray ', ' On Eastnor Knoll ', and ' The Passing Strange ' from ' The Collected Poems of John Masefield ', William Heinemann Ltd.) ; Ingpen & Grant (Edward Thomas) ; John Lane, The Bodley Head Ltd. (A. C. Benson ' The Hawk ' and ' The Phœnix ' from 'Lord Vyet and Other Poems ', John Davidson, ' Earth to Earth ' and ' The Last Journey ' from ' Selected Poems ', Helen Parry Eden, ' Jam Hiems Transiit' from ' Bread and Circuses ') ; the Author and John Lane, The Bodley Head Ltd. (Ford Madox Hueffer, ' When the World was in Building ' and ' When

the World Crumbled ' from ' On Heaven and Other Poems ') ;
Macmillan & Co. Ltd. (Wilfrid Scawen Blunt, ' Esther ' (L),
' Esther ' (LI), ' Satan Absolved ', ' The Mockery of Life ' (I),
' The Mockery of Life ' (II), ' The Mockery of Life ' (III),
and ' The Two Highwaymen ' from ' The Poetical Works
of Wilfrid Scawen Blunt ', Wilfrid Gibson's ' Tenants ' and
' Prometheus ' from ' Collected Poems 1905–1925 ', the
Executors of the late Thomas Hardy for the following
poems by Thomas Hardy, ' The Unborn ', ' God's Funeral ',
' The Last Chrysanthemum ', ' A Plaint to Man ', ' Shelley's
Skylark ', ' To the Moon ', and ' Heredity ', from ' Collected
Poems of Thomas Hardy ', Ralph Hodgson, ' A Song ' and
' The Song of Honour ' from ' Poems ', James Stephens,
' The Centaurs ', ' Deirdre ', and ' The Main-Deep ' from
' Collected Poems ', W. B. Yeats, ' The Man who Dreamed
of Faeryland ', ' Ephemera ', and ' The Indian to his Love '
from ' Early Poems and Stories ', ' The Scholars ', ' The
Fisherman ', and ' In Memory of Alfred Pollexfen ' from
' Later Poems ') ;   Elkin Mathews & Marrot Ltd. (J. E.
Flecker, ' The Bridge of Fire ', Max Weber) ; the Author
and Methuen & Co. Ltd. (G. K. Chesterton, ' The Rolling
English Road ' from ' Wine, Water & Song ') ;   Oxford
University Press (Robert Bridges, The family of the late
Gerard Manley Hopkins, J. D. C. Pellow) ; the Authors
and The Poetry Bookshop (Frances Cornford, F. S. Flint,
Charlotte Mew, Harold Monro, Mary Morison Webster,
Anna Wickham) ; the Authors and Martin Secker Ltd. (Lord
Alfred Douglas, Mrs. J. E. Flecker, Ford Madox Hueffer,
D. H. Lawrence, Viola Meynell, Ezra Pound) ; Sidgwick &
Jackson Ltd. (Edmund Blunden, ' The Pike ' from ' The
Waggoner ', John Drinkwater, ' At an Inn ' from ' Collected
Poems ', W. J. Turner, ' The Lion ' from ' In Time like
Glass ') ; the Literary Executor of the late Rupert Brooke
and Sidgwick & Jackson Ltd. for the following poems by
Rupert Brooke, ' Heaven ', ' Thoughts on the Shape of
the Human Body ', ' The Funeral of Youth : Threnody,'
and ' The Hill ' from ' Collected Poems '; G. D. Day, Esq.,
and Sidgwick & Jackson Ltd. for Jeffery Day, ' On the

14

Wings of the Morning' from 'Poems and Rhymes', and to the following Authors whose personal permission was obtained :—Lascelles Abercrombie, John Alford, Lawrence Binyon, Roy Campbell, Padraic Colum, H. D., Walter de la Mare (' Napoleon ', ' Echo ', ' The Moth ', ' Queen Djenira '), Vivian Locke Ellis, Mrs. G. M. P. Welby Everard (Literary Executor of Maurice Hewlett), the late John Freeman, Robert Graves, A. E. Housman, James Joyce, R. A. K. Mason, T. Sturge Moore, (and on behalf of Michael Field), Sir Henry Newbolt, H. D. C. Pepler, Eden Phillpotts, Herbert Read (on behalf of T. E. Hulme), Siegfried Sassoon, Fredegond Shove, J. C. Squire, W. J. Turner, Humbert Wolfe.

THE order of the poems has been arranged by the Editor. Where two or more poems by the same author appear in sequence, the name of the author is given only at the head of the first of the group. This does not however imply that the author is not represented elsewhere.

I

HIGH on the bridge of Heaven whose Eastern bars
Exclude the interchange of Night and Day,
Robed with faint seas and crowned with quiet stars
All great Gods dwell to whom men prayed or pray.
No winter chills, no fear or fever mars
Their grand and timeless hours of pomp and play;
Some drive about the Rim wind-golden cars
Or, shouting, laugh Eternity away.
       The daughters of their pride,
       Moon-pale, blue-water-eyed,
Their flame-white bodies pearled with failing spray,
       Send all their dark hair streaming
       Down where the worlds lie gleaming,
And draw their mighty lovers close and say :
       " Come over by the Stream ; one hears
The speech of Nations broken in the chant of Spheres."

II

Hear now the song of those bright Shapes that shine
Huge as Leviathans, tasting the fare
Delicate-sweet, while scented dews divine
Thrill from the ground and clasp the rosy air,
" Sing on, sing out, and reach a hand for wine,
For the brown small Earth is softly afloat down there,
And the suns burn low, and the sky is sapphirine,
And the little winds of space are in our hair—
       The little winds of space
       Blow in the love-god's face,
The only god who lacks not praise and prayer ;
       He shall preserve his powers
       Though Ruin shake square towers
And echoing Temples fall without repair,
       And still go forth as strong as ten,
A red immortal riding in the hearts of men ! "

The Gods whose faces are the morning light
Of they who love the leafy rood of song,
The Gods of Greece, dividing the broad night,
Have gathered on the Bridge, of all that throng
The fairest, whether he whose feet for flight
Had plumy wings, or she to whom belong
Shadows, Persephone, or that swan-white
Rose-breasted island lady, gentle and strong,
      Or younger gods than these
      That peep among the trees
And dance when Dionysus beats his gong,
      Or the old disastrous gods
      That nod with snaky nods
Brandishing high the sharp and triple thong,
      Or whom the dull profound of Hell
Spits forth, the reeling Typhon that in dark must dwell.

IV

Shadows there are that seem to look for home
Each spreading like a gloom across the plain,
Voiced like a great bell swinging in a dome,
Appealing mightily for realms to reign.
They were the slow and shapeless gods of Rome,
Laborious gods, who founded power on pain,
These watched the peasant turn his sullen loam,
These drave him out to fight, nor drave in vain :
      Saturnus white and old
      Who lost the age of gold,
Mars who was proud to stand on the deep-piled slain,
      Pomona from whose womb
      Slow fruits in season come,
And, tower-crowned mother of the yellow grain,
      Demeter, and the avenging dead,
The silent Lemures, in fear with honey fed.

Belus and Ra and that most jealous Lord
Who rolled the hosts of Pharaoh in the sea,
Trolls of the North, in every hand a sword,
Gnomes and dwarfs and the shuddering company,
Gods who take vengeance, gods who grant reward,
Gods who exact a murdered devotee,
Brahma the kind, and Siva the abhorred
And they who tend Ygdrasil, the big tree,
   And Isis, the young moon,
   And she of the piping tune,
Her Phrygian sister, cruel Cybele,
   Orpheus the lone harp-player
   And Mithras the man-slayer,
And Allah rumbling on to victory,
  And some, the oldest of them all,
Square heads that leer and lust, and lizard shapes that
 crawl.

VI

Between the pedestals of Night and Morning,
Between red death and radiant desire
With not one sound of triumph or of warning
Stands the great sentry on the Bridge of Fire.
O transient soul, thy thought with dreams adorning,
Cast down the laurel, and unstring the lyre :
The wheels of Time are turning, turning, turning,
The slow stream channels deep and doth not tire.
   Gods on their Bridge above
   Whispering lies and love
Shall mock your passage down the sunless river
   Which, rolling all its streams,
   Shall take you, king of dreams,
—Unthroned and unapproachable for ever—
  To where the kings who dreamed of old
Whiten in habitations monumental cold.

SWEET STAY-AT-HOME *W. H. Davies*

Sweet Stay-at-Home, sweet Well-content,
Thou knowest of no strange continent:
Thou hast not felt thy bosom keep
A gentle motion with the deep;
Thou hast not sailed in Indian seas,
Where scent comes forth in every breeze.
Thou hast not seen the rich grape grow
For miles, as far as eyes can go;
Thou hast not seen a summer's night
When maids could sew by a worm's light;
Nor the North Sea in spring send out
Bright hues that like birds flit about
In solid cages of white ice—
Sweet Stay-at-Home, sweet Love-one-place.
Thou hast not seen black fingers pick
White cotton when the bloom is thick,
Nor heard black throats in harmony;
Nor hast thou sat on stones that lie
Flat on the earth, that once did rise
To hide proud kings from common eyes,
Thou hast not seen plains full of bloom
Where green things had such little room
They pleased the eye like fairer flowers—
Sweet Stay-at-Home, all these lone hours.
Sweet Well-content, sweet Love-one-place,
Sweet, simple maid, bless thy dear face;
For thou hast made more homely stuff
Nurture thy gentle self enough;
I love thee for a heart that's kind—
Not for the knowledge in thy mind.

FISH (fly-replete, in depth of June,
Dawdling away their wat'ry noon)
Ponder deep wisdom, dark or clear,
Each secret fishy hope or fear.
Fish say, they have their Stream and Pond;
But is there anything Beyond?
This life cannot be All, they swear,
For how unpleasant, if it were!
One may not doubt that, somehow, Good
Shall come of Water and of Mud;
And, sure, the reverent eye must see
A Purpose in Liquidity.
We darkly know, by Faith we cry,
The future is not Wholly Dry.
Mud unto mud!—Death eddies near—
Not here the appointed End, not here!
But somewhere, beyond Space and Time,
Is wetter water, slimier slime!
And there (they trust) there swimmeth One
Who swam ere rivers were begun,
Immense, of fishy form and mind,
Squamous, omnipotent, and kind;
And under that Almighty Fin,
The littlest fish may enter in.
Oh! never fly conceals a hook,
Fish say, in the Eternal Brook,
But more than mundane weeds are there,
And mud, celestially fair;
Fat caterpillars drift around,
And Paradisal grubs are found;
Unfading moths, immortal flies,
And the worm that never dies.
And in that Heaven of all their wish,
There shall be no more land, say fish.

THE LINNET *Robert Bridges*

I HEARD a linnet courting
  His lady in the spring :
His mates were idly sporting,
  Nor stayed to hear him sing
    His song of love.—
I fear my speech distorting
    His tender love.

The phrases of his pleading
  Were full of young delight ;
And she that gave him heeding
  Interpreted aright
    His gay, sweet notes,—
So sadly marred in the reading,—
    His tender notes.

And when he ceased, the hearer
  Awaited the refrain,
Till swiftly perching nearer
  He sang his song again,
    His pretty song :—
Would that my verse spake clearer
    His tender song !

Ye happy, airy creatures !
  That in the merry spring
Think not of what misfeatures
  Or cares the year may bring ;
    But unto love
Resign your simple natures
    To tender love.

20TH CENTURY POETRY

An anthology made by HAROLD MONRO

4th Large Impression

'HAROLD MONRO is . . . an excellent anthologist. When the new poetry gets itself on the map, he will be entitled to count among the chief cartographers. I like his short preface. In it he duly announces that this anthology has not been compiled from other anthologies, and that he has read or re-read 600 volumes for the compiling of it... I have been much impressed by *Twentieth Century Poetry*. I read it with increasing respect and pleasure ... on the whole its contents are surprisingly beautiful. There are more good poets around than I had supposed.

Twentieth Century Poetry is the best anthology of the moderns that I have seen.' ARNOLD BENNETT in *The Evening Standard*

'IT surprises the reader with a new sense of the riches of his own times.' *The Times Literary Supplement*

'EASILY the best of the anthologies of modern verse is *Twentieth Century Poetry*, chosen by Harold Monro, himself a poet of rare distinction . . . the product of a wide and diligent investigation of all the original sources. The brief introduction strikes me as a really profound piece of criticism.' *The Morning Post*

'HE has given us a new and fully representative anthology of modern poetry. "May it delight you" is the parting valediction of his preface. It does.' *The Glasgow Herald*

'AN individual and refreshingly alert collection, full of small shocks and pleasant surprises, such as make the chief justification of anthologies. There is none of the Olympian integrity of the "Golden Treasury" here, but a stimulating concatenation of contemporary verse.' *Time and Tide*

*

PHOENIX LIBRARY
3s. 6d. net (cloth) and 5s. net (leather)

(Postage 3d.)

Of all booksellers

CHATTO & WINDUS

97 & 99 St. Martin's Lane, London, W.C.2

DULCE ET DECORUM EST *Wilfred Owen*

BENT double, like old beggars under sacks,
Knock-kneed, coughing like hags, we cursed through
    sludge,
Till on the haunting flares we turned our backs,
And towards our distant rest began to trudge.
Men marched asleep. Many had lost their boots,
But limped on, blood-shod. All went lame, all blind;
Drunk with fatigue; deaf even to the hoots
Of gas-shells dropping softly behind.

Gas! GAS! Quick, boys!—An ecstasy of fumbling
Fitting the clumsy helmets just in time,
But someone still was yelling out and stumbling
And flound'ring like a man in fire or lime,—
Dim through the misty panes and thick green light,
As under a green sea, I saw him drowning.

In all my dreams before my helpless sight
He plunges at me, guttering, choking, drowning.

If in some smothering dreams, you too could pace
Behind the wagon that we flung him in,
And watch the white eyes writhing in his face,
His hanging face, like a devil's sick of sin,
If you could hear, at every jolt, the blood
Come gargling from the froth-corrupted lungs
Bitten as the cud
Of vile, incurable sores on innocent tongues,—
My friend, you would not tell with such high zest
To children ardent for some desperate glory,
The old Lie : *Dulce et decorum est
Pro patria mori.*

WHERE the region grows without a lord,
  Between the thickets emerald-stoled,
In the woodland bottom the virgin sward,
   The cream of the earth, through depths of mold
     O'erflowing wells from secret cells,
While the moon and the sun keep watch and ward,
   And the ancient world is never old.

Here, alone, by the grass-green hearth
  Tarry a little : the mood will come !
Feel your body a part of earth ;
   Rest and quicken your thought at home ;
     Take your ease with the brooding trees ;
Join in their deep-down silent mirth
   The crumbling rock and the fertile loam.

Listen and watch ! The wind will sing ;
  And the day go out by the western gate ;
The night come up on her darkling wing ;
  And the stars with flaming torches wait.
     Listen and see ! And love and be
The day and the night and the world-wide thing
  Of strength and hope you contemplate.

No lofty Patron of Nature ! No ;
  Nor a callous devotee of Art !
But the friend and the mate of the high and the low,
  And the pal to take the vermin's part,
     Your inmost thought divinely wrought,
In the grey earth of your brain aglow
  With the red earth burning in your heart.

24

HE who has once been happy is for aye
  Out of destruction's reach. His fortune then
Holds nothing secret, and Eternity,
  Which is a mystery to other men,
Has like a woman given him its joy,
  Time is his conquest. Life, if it should fret,
Has paid him tribute. He can bear to die.
  He who has once been happy! When I set
The world before me and survey its range,
  Its mean ambitions, its scant fantasies,
The shreds of pleasure which for lack of change
  Men wrap around them and call happiness,
The poor delights which are the tale and sum
Of the world's courage in its martyrdom;

ESTHER (LI)

WHEN I hear laughter from a tavern door,
  When I see crowds agape and in the rain
Watching on tiptoe and with stifled roar
  To see a rocket fired or a bull slain,
When misers handle gold, when orators
  Touch strong men's hearts with glory till they weep,
When cities deck their streets for barren wars
  Which have laid waste their youth, and when I keep
Calmly the count of my own life and see
  On what poor stuff my manhood's dreams were fed
Till I too learned what dole of vanity
  Will serve a human soul for daily bread,
—Then I remember that I once was young
And lived with Esther the world's gods among.

25

THE UNBORN *Thomas Hardy*

I ROSE at night, and visited
  The Cave of the Unborn :
And crowding shapes surrounded me
For tidings of the life to be,
Who long had prayed the silent Head
  To haste its advent morn.

Their eyes were lit with artless trust,
  Hope thrilled their every tone ;
" A scene the loveliest, is it not ?
A pure delight, a beauty-spot
Where all is gentle, true and just,
  And darkness is unknown ? "

My heart was anguished for their sake,
  I could not frame a word ;
And they descried my sunken face,
And seemed to read therein, and trace
The news that pity would not break,
  Nor truth leave unaverred.

And as I silently retired
  I turned and watched them still,
And they came helter-skelter out,
Driven forward like a rabble rout
Into the world they had so desired,
  By the all-immanent Will.

SEHNSUCHT *Anna Wickham*

BECAUSE of body's hunger are we born,
And by contriving hunger are we fed ;
Because of hunger is our work well done,
As so are songs well sung, and things well said.
Desire and longing are the whips of God—
God save us all from death when we are fed.

26

PIED BEAUTY

Gerard Manley Hopkins

GLORY be to God for dappled things—
  For skies of couple-colour as a brinded cow ;
    For rose-moles all in stipple upon trout that swim ;
Fresh-firecoal chestnut-falls ; finches' wings ;
  Landscape plotted and pieced—fold, fallow, and plough ;
    And áll trádes, their gear and tackle and trim.

All things counter, original, spare, strange ;
  Whatever is fickle, freckled (who knows how ?)
    With swift, slow ; sweet, sour ; adazzle, dim ;
He fathers-forth whose beauty is past change :
          Praise him.

THE STARLIGHT NIGHT

LOOK at the stars ! look, look up at the skies !
  O look at all the fire-folk sitting in the air !
  The bright boroughs, the circle-citadels there !
Down in dim woods the diamond delves ! the elves'-
    eyes !
The grey lawns cold where gold, where quickgold lies !
  Wind-beat whitebeam ! airy abeles set on a flare !
  Flake-doves sent floating forth at a farmyard scare !—
Ah well ! it is all a purchase, all is a prize.

Buy then ! bid then !—What ?—Prayer, patience, alms,
    vows.
Look, look : a May-mess, like on orchard boughs !
  Look ! March-bloom, like on mealed-with-yellow
    sallows !
These are indeed the barn ; withindoors house
The shocks. This piece-bright paling shuts the spouse
  Christ home, Christ and his mother and all his hallows.

THE FARMER, 1917 *Fredegond Shove*

I SEE a farmer walking by himself
In the ploughed field, returning like the day
To his dark nest. The plovers circle round
In the gray sky ; the blackbird calls ; the thrush
Still sings—but all the rest have gone to sleep.
I see the farmer coming up the field,
Where the new corn is sown, but not yet sprung ;
He seems to be the only man alive
And thinking through the twilight of this world.
I know that there is war behind those hills,
And I surmise, but cannot see the dead,
And cannot see the living in their midst—
So awfully and madly knit with death.
I cannot feel, but know that there is war,
And has been now for three eternal years,
Behind the subtle cinctures of those hills.
I see the farmer coming up the field,
And as I look, imagination lifts
The sullen veil of alternating cloud,
And I am stunned by what I see behind
His solemn and uncompromising form :
Wide hosts of men who once could walk like him
In freedom, quite alone with night and day,
Uncounted shapes of living flesh and bone,
Worn dull, quenched dry, gone blind and sick, with war ;
And they are him and he is one with them ;
They see him as he travels up the field.
O God, how lonely freedom seems to-day !
O single farmer walking through the world,
They bless the seed in you that earth shall reap,
When they, their countless lives, and all their thoughts,
Lie scattered by the storm : when peace shall come
With stillness, and long shivers, after death.

'MY DELIGHT AND THY DELIGHT'

Robert Bridges

My delight and thy delight
Walking, like two angels white,
In the gardens of the night:

My desire and thy desire
Twining to a tongue of fire,
Leaping live, and laughing higher;
Thro' the everlasting strife
In the mystery of life.

Love, from whom the world begun,
Hath the secret of the sun.

Love can tell, and love alone,
Whence the million stars were strewn,
Why each atom knows its own,
How, in spite of woe and death,
Gay is life, and sweet is breath:

This he taught us, this we knew,
Happy in his science true,
Hand in hand as we stood
Neath the shadows of the wood,
Heart to heart as we lay
In the dawning of the day.

THE MAN WHO DREAMED OF FAERYLAND

W. B. Yeats

He stood among a crowd at Drumahair ;
His heart hung all upon a silken dress,
And he had known at last some tenderness,
Before earth made of him her sleepy care ;
But when a man poured fish into a pile,
It seemed they raised their little silver heads,
And sang how day a Druid twilight sheds
Upon a dim, green, well-beloved isle,
Where people love beside star-laden seas ;
How Time may never mar their faery vows
Under the woven roofs of quicken boughs :
The singing shook him out of his new ease.

He wandered by the sands of Lisadill ;
His mind ran all on money cares and fears,
And he had known at last some prudent years
Before they heaped his grave under the hill ;
But while he passed before a plashy place,
A lug-worm with its grey and muddy mouth
Sang how somewhere to north or west or south
There dwelt a gay, exulting, gentle race ;
And how beneath those three times blessed skies
A Danaan fruitage makes a shower of moons,
And as it falls awakens leafy tunes :
And at that singing he was no more wise.

He mused beside the well of Scanavin,
He mused upon his mockers : without fail
His sudden vengeance were a country tale,
Now that deep earth has drunk his body in ;
But one small knot-grass growing by the pool
Told where, ah, little, all-unneeded voice !
Old Silence bids a lonely folk rejoice,

And chaplet their calm brows with leafage cool,
And how, when fades the sea-strewn rose of day,
A gentle feeling wraps them like a fleece,
And all their trouble dies into its peace :
The tale drove his fine angry mood away.

He slept under the hill of Lugnagall ;
And might have known at last unhaunted sleep
Under that cold and vapour-turbaned steep,
Now that old earth had taken man and all :
Were not the worms that spired about his bones
Proclaiming with a low and reedy cry,
That God had leaned His hands out of the sky,
To bless that isle with honey in His tones ;
That none may feel the power of squall and wave
And no one any leaf-crowned dancer miss
Until He burn up Nature with a kiss :
The man has found no comfort in the grave.

THE SCHOLARS

BALD heads forgetful of their sins,
Old, learned, respectable bald heads
Edit and annotate the lines
That young men, tossing on their beds,
Rhymed out in love's despair
To flatter beauty's ignorant ear.

They'll cough in the ink to the world's end ;
Wear out the carpet with their shoes
Earning respect ; have no strange friend ;
If they have sinned nobody knows.
Lord, what would they say
Should their Catullus walk that way ?

THE HOLLOW MEN

T. S. Eliot

A penny for the Old Guy

I

WE are the hollow men
We are the stuffed men
Leaning together
Headpiece filled with straw. Alas !
Our dried voices, when
We whisper together
Are quiet and meaningless
As wind in dry grass
Or rats' feet over broken glass
In our dry cellar

Shape without form, shade without colour,
Paralysed force, gesture without motion ;

Those who have crossed
With direct eyes, to death's other Kingdom
Remember us—if at all—not as lost
Violent souls, but only
As the hollow men
The stuffed men.

II

Eyes I dare not meet in dreams
In death's dream kingdom
These do not appear :
There, the eyes are
Sunlight on a broken column
There, is a tree swinging

And voices are
In the wind's singing
More distant and more solemn
Than a fading star.

Let me be no nearer
In death's dream kingdom
Let me also wear
Such deliberate disguises—
Rat's coat, crowskin, crossed staves
In a field
Behaving as the wind behaves
No nearer—

Not that final meeting
In the twilight kingdom.

III

This is the dead land
This is cactus land
Here the stone images
Are raised, here they receive
The supplication of a dead man's hand
Under the twinkle of a fading star.

Is it like this
In death's other kingdom?
Waking alone
At the hour when we are
Trembling with tenderness,
Lips that would kiss
Form prayers to broken stone.

C

The eyes are not here
There are no eyes here
In this valley of dying stars,
In this hollow valley
This broken jaw of our lost kingdoms

In this last of meeting places
We grope together
And avoid speech
Gathered on this beach of the tumid river

Sightless, unless
The eyes reappear
As the perpetual star
And multifoliate rose
Of death's twilight kingdom
The only hope
Of empty men.

V

Here we go round the prickly pear
Prickly pear prickly pear
Here we go round the prickly pear
At five o'clock in the morning.

Between the idea
And the reality
Between the motion
And the act
Falls the Shadow

             For Thine is the Kingdom

Between the conception
And the creation
Between the emotion
And the response
Falls the Shadow

Life is very long

Between the desire
And the spasm,
Between the potency
And the existence
Between the essence
And the descent
Falls the Shadow.

For Thine is the Kingdom

For Thine is
Life is
For Thine is the

This is the way the world ends
This is the way the world ends
This is the way the world ends
Not with a bang but a whimper.

A SONG

Ralph Hodgson

WITH Love among the haycocks
We played at hide and seek ;

He shut his eyes and counted—
We hid among the hay—
Then he a haycock mounted,
And spied us where we lay ;

And O ! the merry laughter
Across the hayfield after !

Thou that wast once my loved and loving friend,
A friend no more, I had forgot thee quite,
Why hast thou come to trouble my delight
With memories ? Oh ! I had clean made end
Of all that time, I had made haste to send
My soul into red places, and to light
A torch of pleasure to burn up my night.
What I have woven hast thou come to rend ?

In silent acres of forgetful flowers,
Crowned as of old with happy daffodils,
Long time my wounded soul has been a-straying,
Alas ! it has chanced now on sombre hours
Of hard remembrances and sad delaying
Leaving green valleys for the bitter hills.

THE UNSPEAKABLE ENGLISHMAN

You were a brute and more than half a knave,
Your mind was seamed with labyrinthine tracks
Wherein walked crazy moods bending their backs
Under grim loads. You were an open grave
For gold and love. Always you were the slave
Of crooked thoughts (tortured upon the racks
Of mean mistrust). I made myself as wax
To your fierce seal. I clutched an ebbing wave.

Fool that I was, I loved you ; your harsh soul
Was sweet to me : I gave you with both hands
Love, service, honour, loyalty and praise ;
I would have died for you ! And like a mole
You grubbed and burrowed till the shifting sands
Opened and swallowed up the dream-forged days.

36

Eden Phillpotts

By the abortions of the teeming Spring,
By Summer's starved and withered offering,
By Autumn's stricken hope and Winter's sting,
Oh, hear !

By the ichneumon on the writhing worm,
By the swift far-flung poison of the germ,
By soft and foul brought out of hard and firm,
Oh, hear !

By the fierce battle under every blade,
By the etiolation of the shade,
By drought and thirst and things undone half made,
Oh, hear !

By all the horrors of re-quickened dust,
By the eternal waste of baffled lust,
By mildews and by cankers and by rust,
Oh, hear !

By the fierce scythe of Spring upon the wold,
By the dead eaning mother in the fold,
By stillborn, stricken young and tortured old,
Oh, hear !

By fading eyes pecked from a dying head,
By the hot mouthful of a thing not dead,
By all thy bleeding, struggling, shrieking red,
Oh, hear !

By all the agonies of all the past,
By earth's cold dust and ashes at the last,
By her return to the unconscious vast,
Oh, hear !

37

THE OLD SHIPS

J. E. Flecker

I HAVE seen old ships sail like swans asleep
Beyond the village which men still call Tyre,
With leaden age o'ercargoed, dipping deep
For Famagusta and the hidden sun
That rings black Cyprus with a lake of fire ;
And all those ships were certainly so old
Who knows how oft with squat and noisy gun,
Questing brown slaves or Syrian oranges,
The pirate Genoese
Hell-raked them till they rolled
Blood, water, fruit and corpses up the hold.
But now through friendly seas they softly run,
Painted the mid-sea blue or shore-sea green,
Still patterned with the vine and grapes in gold.

But I have seen
Pointing her shapely shadows from the dawn
And image tumbled on a rose-swept bay,
A drowsy ship of some yet older day ;
And, wonder's breath indrawn,
Thought I—who knows—who knows—but in that same
(Fished up beyond Æææ, patched up new
—Stern painted brighter blue—)
That talkative, bald-headed seaman came
(Twelve patient comrades sweating at the oar)
From Troy's doom-crimson shore,
And with great lies about his wooden horse
Set the crew laughing, and forgot his course.

It was so old a ship—who knows, who knows ?
—And yet so beautiful, I watched in vain
To see the mast burst open with a rose,
And the whole deck put on its leaves again.

GOD'S FUNERAL *Thomas Hardy*

I

I SAW a slowly-stepping train—
Lined on the brows, scoop-eyed and bent and hoar—
Following in files across a twilit plain
A strange and mystic form the foremost bore.

II

And by contagious throbs of thought
Or latent knowledge that within me lay
And had already stirred me, I was wrought
To consciousness of sorrow even as they.

III

The fore-borne shape, to my blurred eyes,
At first seemed man-like, and anon to change
To an amorphous cloud of marvellous size,
At times endowed with wings of glorious range.

IV

And this phantasmal variousness
Ever possessed it as they drew along :
Yet throughout all it symboled none the less
Potency vast and loving-kindness strong.

V

Almost before I knew I bent
Towards the moving columns without a word ;
They, growing in bulk and numbers as they went,
Struck out sick thoughts that could be overheard :—

" O man-projected Figure, of late
Imaged as we, thy knell who shall survive ?
Whence came it we were tempted to create
One whom we can no longer keep alive ?

VII

" Framing him jealous, fierce, at first,
We gave him justice as the ages rolled,
Will to bless those by circumstance accurst,
And longsuffering, and mercies manifold.

VIII

" And, tricked by our own early dream
And need of solace, we grew self-deceived,
Our making soon our maker did we deem,
And what we had imagined we believed.

IX

" Till, in Time's stayless stealthy swing,
Uncompromising rude reality
Mangled the Monarch of our fashioning,
Who quavered, sank ; and now has ceased to be.

X

" So, toward our myth's oblivion,
Darkling, and languid-lipped, we creep and grope
Sadlier than those who wept in Babylon,
Whose Zion was a still abiding hope.

XI

" How sweet it was in years far hied
To start the wheels of day with trustful prayer,
To lie down liegely at the eventide
And feel a blest assurance he was there !

XII

" And who or what shall fill his place ?
Whither will wanderers turn distracted eyes
For some fixed star to stimulate their pace
Towards the goal of their enterprise ? " . . .

XIII

Some in the background then I saw,
Sweet women, youths, men, all incredulous,
Who chimed : " This is a counterfeit of straw,
This requiem mockery ! Still he lives to us ! "

XIV

I could not buoy their faith : and yet
Many I had known : with all I sympathized ;
And though struck speechless, I did not forget
That what was mourned for, I, too, long had prized.

XV

Still, how to bear such loss I deemed
The insistent question for each animate mind,
And gazing, to my growing sight there seemed
A pale yet positive gleam low down behind,

XVI

Whereof, to lift the general night,
A certain few who stood aloof had said,
" See you upon the horizon that small light—
Swelling somewhat ? " Each mourner shook his head.

XVII

And they composed a crowd of whom
Some were right good, and many nigh the best. . . .
Thus dazed and puzzled 'twixt the gleam and gloom
Mechanically I followed with the rest.

THE LAST CHRYSANTHEMUM

WHY should this flower delay so long
        To show its tremulous plumes ?
Now is the time of plaintive robin-song,
        When flowers are in their tombs.

Through the slow summer, when the sun
        Called to each frond and whorl
That all he could for flowers was being done,
        Why did it not uncurl ?

It must have felt that fervid call
        Although it took no heed,
Waking but now, when leaves like corpses fall,
        And saps all retrocede.

Too late its beauty, lonely thing,
        The season's shine is spent,
Nothing remains for it but shivering
        In tempests turbulent.

Had it a reason for delay
        Dreaming in witlessness
That for a bloom so delicately gay
        Winter would stay its stress ?

—I talk as if the thing were born
        With sense to work its mind ;
Yet it is but one mask of many worn
        By the Great Face behind.

THE DEAD BIRD *Max Weber*

MOTIONLESS, cold, shrunk thou liest
Thy colour faded, thy once gay feather-garment muti-
    lated,
Thy senses gone, thy pulse stopped,
Thy warm blood cold, thy loving mother-heart stilled,
Thy sharp circumspective moment-glimpsing eyes closed,
Thine upright proud head now drooped and sunk,
Thy quivering sensitive claws now shrivelled and tight
    and numb,
Thy beautiful wings thy greatest power,
Thy beautiful wings thy greatest force,
Thy beautiful wings that carried thee on the winds,
Thy beautiful wings made thee queen of the air and space,
Thy beautiful wings fluttering countless times a moment,
Thy beautiful wings now lie limp and closed.
From thy trees death hath taken thee,
To this lonely and unvisited place.
Thy babes thou untimely left behind thee
Are now in wonder of the everlasting wonder.
I know they cry for thee in thirst and hunger
And in fear they wonder what hath o'ertaken thee.
No more thy song, no more thy laughter,
No more thy call, no more thine answer.
Oh dead silent bird, I hear other birds sing,
With whom in innocent company of thine own kind,
But a while ago thou too hadst sung.
Oh dead bird I hear other birds sing,
Whether 'tis song of glory or song of death,
No one but thou couldst tell me.
Oh dead mute bird I feel thy sisters call thee,
But no one here for thee can answer them,
That their ardent call is in vain.
No one but thou couldst answer them,
That million will come and live after thee.
Oh dead cold mother bird,
Alone dead, here alone thou liest.

Thy sisters sing and in glory sing and call,
But no more shalt thou return.
Then adieu for thee oh dead bird to a new beginning
Thy life that has been is not ended.
Thy death is but a prelude for another form,
Which only destiny contains,
And thou oh dead bird, as all,
Helpest with thy life and death,
To make for thy rhythmic form of the infinite.
And though dead thou art now,
Thine having been will always be.

THE NIGHTINGALE NEAR THE HOUSE

Harold Monro

Here is the soundless cypress on the lawn :
It listens, listens. Taller trees beyond
Listen. The moon at the unruffled pond
    Stares. And you sing, you sing.

That star-enchanted song falls through the air
From lawn to lawn down terraces of sound,
Darts in white arrows on the shadowed ground ;
    While all the night you sing.

My dreams are flowers to which you are a bee,
As all night long I listen, and my brain
Receives your song, then loses it again
    In moonlight on the lawn.

Now is your voice a marble high and white,
Then like a mist on fields of paradise ;
Now is a raging fire, then is like ice,
    Then breaks, and it is dawn.

THE YARN OF THE *LOCH ACHRAY*

John Masefield

THE *Loch Achray* was a clipper tall
With seven-and-twenty hands in all.
Twenty to hand and reef and haul,
A skipper to sail and mates to bawl
" Tally on to the tackle-fall,
Heave now 'n' start her, heave 'n' pawl ! "
      Hear the yarn of a sailor,
      An old yarn learned at sea.

Her crew were shipped and they said " Farewell,
So-long, my Tottie, my lovely gell ;
We sail to-day if we fetch to hell,
It's time we tackled the wheel a spell."
      Hear the yarn of a sailor,
      An old yarn learned at sea.

The dockside loafers talked on the quay
The day that she towed down to sea :
" Lord, what a handsome ship she be !
Cheer her, sonny boys, three times three ! "
And the dockside loafers gave her a shout
As the red-funnelled tug-boat towed her out ;
They gave her a cheer as the custom is,
And the crew yelled " Take our loves to Liz—
Three cheers, bullies, for old Pier Head
'N' the bloody stay-at-homes ! " they said.
      Hear the yarn of a sailor,
      An old yarn learned at sea.

In the grey of the coming on of night
She dropped the tug at the Tuskar Light,
'N' the topsails went to the topmast head
To a chorus that fairly awoke the dead.

45

She trimmed her yards and slanted South
With her royals set and a bone in her mouth.
    Hear the yarn of a sailor,
    An old yarn learned at sea.

She crossed the Line and all went well,
They ate, they slept, and they struck the bell
And I give you a gospel truth when I state
The crowd didn't find any fault with the Mate,
But one night off the River Plate.
    Hear the yarn of a sailor,
    An old yarn learned at sea.

It freshened up till it blew like thunder
And burrowed her deep, lee-scuppers under.
The old man said, " I mean to hang on
Till her canvas busts or her sticks are gone "—
Which the blushing looney did, till at last
Overboard went her mizzen-mast.
    Hear the yarn of a sailor,
    An old yarn learned at sea.

Then a fierce squall struck the *Loch Achray*
And bowed her down to her water-way ;
Her main-shrouds gave and her forestay,
And a green sea carried her wheel away ;
Ere the watch below had time to dress
She was cluttered up in a blushing mess.
    Hear the yarn of a sailor,
    An old yarn learned at sea.

She couldn't lay-to nor yet pay-off,
And she got swept clean in the bloody trough ;
Her masts were gone, and afore you knowed
She filled by the head and down she goed.
Her crew made seven-and-twenty dishes

For the big jack-sharks and the little fishes,
And over their bones the water swishes.
    Hear the yarn of a sailor,
    An old yarn learned at sea.

The wives and girls they watch in the rain
For a ship as won't come home again.
" I reckon it's them head-winds," they say,
" She'll be home to-morrow, if not to-day.
I'll just nip home 'n' I'll air the sheets
'N' buy the fixins 'n' cook the meats
As my man likes 'n' as my man eats."

So home they goes by the windy streets,
Thinking their men are homeward bound
With anchors hungry for English ground,
And the bloody fun of it is, they're drowned.
    Hear the yarn of a sailor,
    An old yarn learned at sea.

ON EASTNOR KNOLL

SILENT are the woods, and the dim green boughs are
Hushed in the twilight : yonder in the path through
The apple orchard, is a tired plough-boy
Calling the cows home.

A bright white star blinks, the pale moon rounds, but
Still the red, lurid wreckage of the sunset
Smoulders in smoky fire, and burns on
The misty hill-tops.

Ghostly it grows, and darker, the burning
Fades into smoke, and now the gusty oaks are
A silent army of phantoms thronging
A land of shadows.

My face is against the grass—the moorland grass is wet—
　My eyes are shut against the grass, against my lips
　　there are the little blades,
　　　Over my head the curlews call,
　And now there is the night wind in my hair;
My heart is against the grass and the sweet earth;—it
　　has gone still, at last.
　　　It does not want to beat any more,
　　　　And why should it beat?
　　　This is the end of the journey;
　　　　The Thing is found.

　　　This is the end of all the roads—
　　Over the grass there is the night-dew
And the wind that drives up from the sea along the
　　moorland road;
　　I hear a curlew start out from the heath
　　And fly off, calling through the dusk,
　　　The wild, long, rippling call.
　　The Thing is found and I am quiet with the earth.
Perhaps the earth will hold it, or the wind, or that bird's
　　cry,
But it is not for long in any life I know. This cannot
　　stay,
Not now, not yet, not in a dying world, with me, for
　　very long.
　　　　I leave it here:
　　　And one day the wet grass may give it back—
　　　One day the quiet earth may give it back—
　　The calling birds may give it back as they go by—
To someone walking on the moor who starves for love
　　and will not know
　　　Who gave it to all these to give away;
　　　Or, if I come and ask for it again,
　　　　Oh! then, to me.

THOUGHTS ON THE SHAPE OF THE HUMAN BODY

Rupert Brooke

How can we find ? how can we rest ? how can
We, being gods, win joy, or peace, being man ?
We, the gaunt zanies of a witless Fate,
Who love the unloving, and the lover hate,
Forget the moment ere the moment slips,
Kiss with blind lips that seek beyond the lips,
Who want, and know not what we want, and cry
With crooked mouths for Heaven, and throw it by.
Love's for completeness ! No perfection grows
'Twixt leg, and arm, elbow, and ear, and nose,
And joint, and socket ; but unsatisfied
Sprawling desires, shapeless, perverse, denied.
Finger with finger wreathes ; we love, and gape,
Fantastic shape to mazed fantastic shape,
Straggling, irregular, perplexed, embossed,
Grotesquely twined, extravagantly lost
By crescive paths and strange protuberant ways
From sanity and from wholeness and from grace.
How can love triumph, how can solace be,
Where fever turns toward fever, knee toward knee ?
Could we but fill to harmony, and dwell
Simple as our thought and as perfectible,
Rise disentangled from humanity
Strange whole and new into simplicity,
Grow to a radiant round love, and bear
Unfluctuant passion for some perfect sphere,
Love moon to moon unquestioning, and be
Like the star Lunisequa, steadfastly
Following the round clear orb of her delight,
Patiently ever, through the eternal night !

TO ANY POET

Alice Meynell

Thou who singest through the earth
All the earth's wild creatures fly thee ;
Everywhere thou marrest mirth,—
    Dumbly they defy thee ;
There is something they deny thee.

Pines thy fallen nature ever
For the unfallen Nature sweet.
But she shuns thy long endeavour,
    Though her flowers and wheat
Throng and press thy pausing feet.

Though thou tame a bird to love thee,
Press thy face to grass and flowers,
All these things reserve above thee
    Secrets in the bowers,
Secrets in the sun and showers.

Sing thy sorrow, sing thy gladness,
In thy songs must wind and tree
Bear the fictions of thy sadness,
    Thy humanity.
For their truth is not for thee.

Wait, and many a secret nest,
Many a hoarded winter-store
Will be hidden on thy breast.
    Things thou longest for
Will not fear or shun thee more.

Thou shalt intimately lie
In the roots of flowers that thrust
Upwards from thee to the sky,
    With no more distrust
When they blossom from thy dust.

Silent labours of the rain
Shall be near thee, reconciled ;
Little lives of leaves and grain,
    All things shy and wild,
Tell thee secrets, quiet child.

Earth, set free from thy fair fancies
And the art thou shalt resign,
Will bring forth her rue and pansies
    Unto more divine
Thoughts than any thoughts of thine.

Nought will fear thee, humbled creature.
There will lie thy mortal burden
Pressed unto the heart of Nature,
    Songless in a garden,
With a long embrace of pardon.

Then the truth all creatures tell,
And His will Whom thou entreatest,
Shall absorb thee ; there shall dwell
    Silence, the completest
Of thy poems, last, and sweetest.

THE ROARING FROST

A FLOCK of winds came winging from the North,
Strong birds with fighting pinions driving forth
    With a resounding call :—

Where will they close their wings and cease their cries—
Between what warming seas and conquering skies—
    And fold, and fall ?

ODE TO MUSIC (Extracts)

WRITTEN FOR THE BICENTENARY COMMEMORATION OF HENR PURCELL

Rober **Bridges**

*   *   *

I

  LOVE to Love calleth,
  Love unto Love replieth :
From the ends of the earth, drawn by invisible bands,
Over the dawning and darkening lands
  Love cometh to Love.
  To the pangs of desire ;
To the heart by courage and might
Escaped from hell,
From the torment of raging fire,
From the sighs of the drowning main,
From shipwreck of fear and pain,
From the terror of night.

2

All mankind by Love shall be banded
To combat Evil, the many-handed :
For the spirit of man on beauty feedeth,
The airy fancy he heedeth,
He regardeth Truth in the heavenly height,
In changeful pavilions of loveliness dight,
The sovran sun that knows not the night ;
He loveth the beauty of earth,
And the sweet birds' mirth ;
And out of his heart there falleth
A melody-making river
Of passion, that runneth ever
To the ends of the earth and crieth,
That yearneth and calleth ;

52

And Love from the heart of man
To the heart of man replieth :
    On the wings of desire
    Love cometh to Love.

*   *   *

DIRGE

Man born of desire
Cometh out of the night,
A wandering spark of fire,
A lonely word of eternal thought
Echoing in chance and forgot.

1

He seeth the sun,
He calleth the stars by name,
He saluteth the flowers.—
Wonders of land and sea,
The mountain towers
Of ice and air
He seeth, and calleth them fair :
    Then he hideth his face ;—
Whence he came to pass away
Where all is forgot,
Unmade—lost for aye
With the things that are not.

2

He striveth to know,
To unravel the Mind
That veileth in horror :
He wills to adore.
In wisdom he walketh
And loveth his kind ;
His labouring breath

53

Would keep evermore :
   Then he hideth his face ;—
Whence he came to pass away
Where all is forgot,
Unmade—lost for aye
With the things that are not.

3

   He dreameth of beauty,
He seeks to create
Fairer and fairer
To vanquish his Fate ;
No hindrance he—
No curse will brook,
He maketh a law
No ill shall be :
Then he hideth his face ;—
Whence he came to pass away
Where all is forgot,
Unmade—lost for aye
   With the things that are not.

*   *   *

Rejoice, ye dead, where'er your spirits dwell,
Rejoice that yet on earth your fame is bright,
And that your names, remember'd day and night,
Live on the lips of those who love you well.
  'Tis ye that conquer'd have the powers of Hell
Each with the special grace of your delight ;
Ye are the world's creators, and by might
Alone of Heavenly love ye did excel.
      Now ye are starry names
      Behind the sun ye climb
        To light the glooms of Time
        With deathless flames.

*   *   *

Open for me the gates of delight,
The gates of the garden of man's desire ;
Where spirits touch'd by heavenly fire
    Have planted the trees of life.—
Their branches in beauty are spread,
    Their fruit divine
To the nations is given for bread,
    And crush'd into wine.

*　　*　　*

HUMMING-BIRD   *D. H. Lawrence*

I CAN imagine, in some otherworld
Primeval-dumb, far back
In that most awful stillness, that only gasped and hummed,
Humming-birds raced down the avenues.

Before anything had a soul,
While life was a heave of Matter, half inanimate,
This little bit chipped off in brilliance
And went whizzing through the slow, vast, succulent
    stems.

I believe there were no flowers then,
In the world where the humming-bird flashed ahead of
    creation.
I believe he pierced the slow vegetable veins with his
    long beak.

Probably he was big
As mosses, and little lizards, they say, were once big.
Probably he was a jabbing, terrifying monster.

We look at him through the wrong end of the long
    telescope of Time,
Luckily for us.

LOVE ON THE FARM

WHAT large, dark hands are those at the window
Grasping in the golden light
Which weaves its way through the evening wind
    At my heart's delight ?

Ah, only the leaves ! But in the west
I see a redness suddenly come
Into the evening's anxious breast—
    'Tis the wound of love goes home !

The woodbine creeps abroad
Calling low to her lover :
    The sun-lit flirt who all the day
    Has poised above her lips in play
    And stolen kisses, shallow and gay
    Of pollen, now has gone away—
      She woos the moth with her sweet, low word ;
And when above her his moth-wings hover
Then her bright breast she will uncover
And yield her honey-drop to her lover.

Into the yellow, evening glow
Saunters a man from the farm below ;
Leans, and looks in at the low-built shed
Where the swallow has hung her marriage bed.
    The bird lies warm against the wall.
    She glances quick her startled eyes
    Towards him, then she turns away
    Her small head, making warm display
    Of red upon the throat. Her terrors sway
    Her out of the nest's warm, busy ball,
    Whose plaintive cry is heard as she flies
    In one blue stoop from out the sties
    Into the twilight's empty hall.

56

Oh, water-hen, beside the rushes
Hide your quaintly scarlet blushes,
Still your quick tail, lie still as dead,
Till the distance folds over his ominous tread!

The rabbit presses back her ears,
Turns back her liquid, anguished eyes
And crouches low; then with wild spring
Spurts from the terror of *his* oncoming;
To be choked back, the wire ring
Her frantic effort throttling:
    Piteous brown ball of quivering fears!
Ah, soon in his large, hard hands she dies,
And swings all loose from the swing of his walk!
Yet calm and kindly are his eyes
And ready to open in brown surprise
Should I not answer to his talk
Or should he my tears surmise.

I hear his hand on the latch, and rise from my chair
Watching the door open; he flashes bare
His strong teeth in a smile, and flashes his eyes
In a smile like triumph upon me; then careless-wise
He flings the rabbit soft on the table board
And comes towards me: ah! the uplifted sword
Of his hand against my bosom! and oh, the broad
Blade of his glance that asks me to applaud
His coming! With his hand he turns my face to him
And caresses me with his fingers that still smell grim
Of the rabbit's fur! God, I am caught in a snare!
I know not what fine wire is round my throat;
I only know I let him finger there
My pulse of life, and let him nose like a stoat
Who sniffs with joy before he drinks the blood.

And down his mouth comes to my mouth ! a d dow
His bright dark eyes come over me, like a ho d
Upon my mind ! his lips meet mine, and a ood
Of sweet fire sweeps across me, so I drown
Against him, die, and find death good.

SATAN ABSOLVED
W. S. Blun

(Extract from a Speech of " The Angel of Pity ")

FROM the deep Central Seas
To the white Poles, Man ruleth pitiless Lord of these
And daily he destroyeth. The great whales he driveth
Beneath the northern ice, and quarter none he giveth,
Who perish there of wounds in their huge agony.
He presseth the white bear on the white frozen sea
And slaughtereth for his pastime. The wise amorous
    seal
He flayeth big with young ; the walrus cubs that knee
But cannot turn his rage, alive he mangleth them,
Leaveth in breathing heaps, outrooted branch and stem
In every land he slayeth. He hath new engines made
Which no life may withstand, nor in the forest shade
Nor in the sunlit plain, which wound all from afar,
The timorous with the valiant, waging his false war,
Coward, himself unseen. In pity, Lord, look down
On the blank widowed plains which he hath made his
    own
By right of solitude. Where, Lord God, are they now
Thy glorious bison herds, Thy ariels white as snow,
Thy antelopes in troops, the zebras of Thy plain ?
Behold their whitened bones on the dull track of men.
Thy elephants, Lord, where ? For ages Thou didst build
Their frames' capacity, the hide which was their shield
No thorn might pierce, no sting, no violent tooth assail,
The tusks which were their levers, the lithe trunk their
    flail.

58

Thou strengthenedst their deep brain. Thou madest
    them wise to know
And wiser to ignore, advised, deliberate, slow,
Conscious of power supreme in right. The manifest
    token
Of Thy high will on earth, Thy natural peace unbroken,
Unbreakable by fear. For ages did they move
Thus, kings of Thy deep forest swayed by only love.
Where are they now, Lord God ?

REASON ENOUGH   *T. Sturge Moore*

" Who knows what a man may think ?
To whom do the birds confide
Whether she will have tears to drink
And an hungry heart to hide ?
Come, bandage your eyes,
Give ear though he lies :
For milkmaids and queens and gipsy-princesses
Dream and kiss blindfold or starve upon guesses."

She sang these words and curtseyed : my heart said
That though all heard my face alone was red,—
Though all hands clapped her mine alone kept still,—
Yet I perchance to praise had the best will.
Now sails she, like a spirit taking leave,
Through those glass doors to where the gardens gloom
While dim stars filter through the filmy eve.
Would she walk lonely through sweet solemn places ?
She should be viewed while their spell on her face is ;
Break free, my soul, good manners are thy tomb !

DEAD MAN'S DUMP

Isaac Rosenberg

THE plunging limbers over the shattered track
Racketed with their rusty freight,
Stuck out like many crowns of thorns,
And the rusty stakes like sceptres old
To stay the flood of brutish men
Upon our brothers dear.

The wheels lurched over sprawled dead
But pained them not, though their bones crunched ;
Their shut mouths made no moan,
They lie there huddled, friend and foeman,
Man born of man, and born of woman ;
And shells go crying over them
From night till night and now.

Earth has waited for them,
All the time of their growth
Fretting for their decay :
Now she has them at last !
In the strength of their strength
Suspended—stopped and held.

What fierce imaginings their dark souls lit ?
Earth ! Have they gone into you ?
Somewhere they must have gone,
And flung on your hard back
Is their souls' sack,
Emptied of God-ancestralled essences.
Who hurled them out ? Who hurled ?

None saw their spirits' shadow shake the grass,
Or stood aside for the half used life to pass
Out of those doomed nostrils and the doomed mouth,
When the swift iron burning bee
Drained the wild honey of their youth.

What of us who, flung on the shrieking pyre,
Walk, our usual thoughts untouched,
Our lucky limbs as on ichor fed,
Immortal seeming ever ?
Perhaps when the flames beat loud on us,
A fear may choke in our veins
And the startled blood may stop.

The air is loud with death,
The dark air spurts with fire,
The explosions ceaseless are.
Timelessly now, some minutes past,
These dead strode time with vigorous life,
Till the shrapnel called " An end ! "
But not to all. In bleeding pangs
Some borne on stretchers dreamed of home,
Dear things, war-blotted from their hearts.

A man's brains splattered on
A stretcher-bearer's face ;
His shook shoulders slipped their load,
But when they bent to look again
The drowning soul was sunk too deep
For human tenderness.

They left this dead with the older dead
Stretched at the cross roads.

Burnt black by strange decay
Their sinister faces lie,
The lid over each eye ;
The grass and coloured clay
More motion have than they,

Joined to the great sunk silences.
Here is one not long dead.
His dark hearing caught our far wheels,
And the choked soul stretched weak hands
To reach the living word the far wheels said ;
The blood-dazed intelligence beating for light,
Crying through the suspense of the far torturing wheels
Swift for the end to break
Or the wheels to break,
Cried as the tide of the world broke over his sight,
" Will they come ?   Will they ever come ? "
Even as the mixed hoofs of the mules,
The quivering-bellied mules,
And the rushing wheels all mixed
With his tortured upturned sight.

So we crashed round the bend,
We heard his weak scream,
We heard his very last sound,
And our wheels grazed his dead face.

ON YOUTH STRUCK DOWN   *Charlotte Mew*

(*From an unfinished Elegy*)

OH !   Death what have you to say ?
    " Like a bride—like a bride-groom they ride away :
You shall go back to make up the fire,
To learn patience—to learn grief,
To learn sleep when the light has quite gone out of your
        earthly skies,
But they have the light in their eyes
    To the end of their day."

EPITAPH ON AN ARMY OF MERCENARIES

A. E. Housman

THESE, in the day when heaven was falling,
 The hour when earth's foundations fled,
Followed their mercenary calling
 And took their wages and are dead.

Their shoulders held the sky suspended ;
 They stood, and earth's foundations stay ;
What God abandoned, these defended,
 And saved the sum of things for pay.

A WATER PARTY

Robert Bridges

LET us, as by this verdant bank we float,
Search down the marge to find some shady pool
Where we may rest awhile and moor our boat,
And bathe our tired limbs in the waters cool.
  Beneath the noonday sun,
  Swiftly, O river, run !

Here is a mirror for Narcissus, see !
I cannot sound it, plumbing with my oar.
Lay the stern in beneath this bowering tree !
Now, stepping on this stump, we are ashore.
  Guard, Hamadryades,
  Our clothes laid by your trees !

How the birds warble in the woods ! I pick
The waxen lilies, diving to the root.
But swim not far in the stream, the weeds grow thick,
And hot on the bare head the sunbeams shoot.
  Until our sport be done,
  O merry birds, sing on !

If but to-night the sky be clear, the moon
Will serve us well, for she is near the full.
We shall row safely home ; only too soon,—
So pleasant 'tis, whether we float or pull.
   To guide us through the night,
   O summer moon, shine bright !

EPHEMERA   *W. B. Yeats*

" YOUR eyes that once were never weary of mine
Are bowed in sorrow under pendulous lids,
Because our love is waning."
        And then she :
" Although our love is waning, let us stand
By the lone border of the lake once more,
Together in that hour of gentleness
When the poor tired child, Passion, falls asleep :
How far away the stars seem, and how far
Is our first kiss, and ah, how old my heart ! "

Pensive they paced along the faded leaves,
While slowly he whose hand held hers replied :
" Passion has often worn our wandering hearts."
The woods were round them, and the yellow leaves
Fell like faint meteors in the gloom, and once
A rabbit old and lame limped down the path ;
Autumn was over him : and now they stood
On the lone border of the lake once more :
Turning, he saw that she had thrust dead leaves
Gathered in silence, dewy as her eyes,
In bosom and hair.
     " Ah, do not mourn," he said,
" That we are tired, for other loves await us ;
Hate on and love through unrepining hours.
Before us lies eternity ; our souls
Are love, and a continual farewell."

64

A PLAINT TO MAN

Thomas Hardy

WHEN you slowly emerged from the den of Time,
And gained percipience as you grew,
And fleshed you fair out of shapeless slime,

Wherefore, O Man, did there come to you
The unhappy need of creating me—
A form like your own—for praying to ?

My virtue, power, utility,
Within my maker must all abide,
Since none in myself can ever be,

One thin as a phasm on a lantern-slide
Shown forth in the dark upon some dim sheet,
And by none but its showman vivified.

" Such a forced device," you may say, " is meet
For easing a loaded heart at whiles :
Man needs to conceive of a mercy-seat

Somewhere above the gloomy aisles
Of this wailful world, or he could not bear
The irk no local hope beguiles."

—But since I was framed in your first despair
The doing without me has had no play
In the minds of men when shadows scare ;

And now that I dwindle day by day
Beneath the deicide eyes of seers
In a light that will not let me stay,

And to-morrow the whole of me disappears,
The truth should be told, and the fact be faced
That had best been faced in earlier years :

E

The fact of life with dependence placed
On the human heart's resource alone,
In brotherhood bonded close and graced

With loving-kindness fully blown,
And visioned help unsought, unknown,

John Alford

GLORY, glory to the sun
who spends his being
caring not what he shines upon
nor for whose seeing.

In the furrow swells the wheat
and the chestnut leaf respires,
quickened to life by the heat
of his innocent fires.

Small thanks the farmer allows,
turning his hay,
but watches with reckoning brows
the fall of the day.

Clouds flame in the upper air;
the fields slip to the night;
but the rugged horsemen of Thibet stir
to a finger of light.

They wrap their skins about
and spear in hand,
round up their flocks and shout
and scour the land.

THE WIFE

WE murmured of his kindliness
When by his pit a hundred stood ;
We held him loyal, generous, good,
And only spoke his name to bless.

But, when three years and more were sped,
I came again beside his grave,
And found red dock and darnel wave
Above the unrecorded dead.

His widow listened to my plea,
Then made reply in smouldering tone :
" My master froze my heart to stone ;
That's all the stone he'll get from me ! "

MAN'S DAYS

A SUDDEN wakin', a sudden weepin' ;
A li'l suckin', a li'l sleepin' ;
A cheel's full joys an' a cheel's short sorrows,
Wi' a power o' faith in gert to-morrows.

Young blood red hot an' the love of a maid ;
Wan glorious hour as'll never fade ;
Some shadows, some sunshine, some triumphs, some tears ;
An' a gatherin' weight o' the flyin' years.

Then auld man's talk o' the days behind 'e ;
Your darter's youngest darter to mind 'e ;
A li'l dreamin', a li'l dyin',
A li'l lew corner o' airth to lie in.

RHAPSODY ON A WINDY NIGHT T. S. Eliot

TWELVE o'clock.
Along the reaches of the street
Held in a lunar synthesis,
Whispering lunar incantations
Dissolve the floors of memory
And all its clear relations,
Its divisions and precisions,
Every street lamp that I pass
Beats like a fatalistic drum,
And through the spaces of the dark
Midnight shakes the memory
As a madman shakes a dead geranium.

Half-past one,
The street-lamp sputtered,
The street-lamp muttered,
The street-lamp said, " Regard that woman
Who hesitates toward you in the light of the door
Which opens on her like a grin.
You see the border of her dress
Is torn and stained with sand,
And you see the corner of her eye
Twists like a crooked pin."
The memory throws up high and dry
A crowd of twisted things ;
A twisted branch upon the beach
Eaten smooth, and polished
As if the world gave up
The secret of its skeleton,
Stiff and white.
A broken spring in a factory yard,
Rust that clings to the form that the strength has left
Hard and curled and ready to snap.

Half-past two,
The street-lamp said,
" Remark the cat which flattens itself in the gutter,
Slips out its tongue
And devours a morsel of rancid butter."
So the hand of the child, automatic,
Slipped out and pocketed a toy that was running along
    the quay.
I could see nothing behind that child's eye.
I have seen eyes in the street
Trying to peer through lighted shutters,
And a crab one afternoon in a pool,
An old crab with barnacles on his back,
Gripped the end of a stick which I held him.

Half-past three,
The lamp sputtered,
The lamp muttered in the dark.
The lamp hummed ;
" Regard the moon,
La lune ne garde aucune rancune,
She winks a feeble eye,
She smiles into corners.
She smooths the hair of the grass.
The moon has lost her memory.
A washed-out smallpox cracks her face,
Her hand twists a paper rose,
That smells of dust and eau de Cologne,
She is alone
With all the old nocturnal smells
That cross and cross across her brain."
The reminiscence comes
Of sunless dry geraniums
And dust in crevices,
Smells of chestnuts in the streets,
And female smells in shuttered rooms,
And cigarettes in corridors
And cocktail smells in bars.

The lamp said,
" Four o'clock,
Here is the number on the door.
Memory !
You have the key,
The little lamp spreads a ring on the stair,
Mount.
The bed is open ; the tooth-brush hangs on the wall,
Put your shoes at the door, sleep, prepare for life."

The last twist of the knife.

NOISE OF BATTLE D. H. Lawrence

AND all hours long, the town
   Roars like a beast in a cave
That is wounded there
And like to drown ;
   While days rush, wave after wave
On its lair.

An invisible woe unseals
   The flood, so it passes beyond
All bounds : the great old city
Recumbent roars as it feels
   The foamy paw of the pond
Reach from immensity.

But all that it can do
   Now, as the tide rises,
Is to listen and hear the grim,
Waves crash like thunder through
   The splintered streets, hear noises
Roll hollow in the interim.

ADLESTROP

Edward Thomas

YES. I remember Adlestrop—
The name, because one afternoon
Of heat the express-train drew up there
Unwontedly. It was late June.

The steam hissed. Someone cleared his throat.
No one left and no one came
On the bare platform. What I saw
Was Adlestrop—only the name

And willows, willow-herb, and grass,
And meadowsweet, and haycocks dry,
No whit less still and lonely fair
Than the high cloudlets in the sky.

And for that minute a blackbird sang
Close by, and round him, mistier,
Farther and farther, all the birds
Of Oxfordshire and Gloucestershire.

I BUILT MYSELF A HOUSE OF GLASS

I BUILT myself a house of glass :
It took me years to make it :
And I was proud. But now, alas !
Would God someone would break it.

But it looks too magnificent.
No neighbour casts a stone
From where he dwells, in tenement
Or palace of glass, alone.

71

I

You are clear,
O rose, cut in rock
hard as the descent of hail.

I could scrape the colour
from the petals,
like spilt dye from a rock.

If I could break you
I could break a tree.

If I could stir
I could break a tree,
I could break you.

II

O wind,
rend open the heat,
cut apart the heat,
rend it to tatters.

Fruit cannot drop
through this thick air—
fruit cannot fall into heat
that presses up and blunts
the points of pears
and rounds the grapes.

Cut the heat—
plough through it,
turning it on either side
of your path.

As the young phœnix, duteous to his sire,
Lifts in his beak the creature he has been,
And lifting o'er the corse broad vans for screen,
Bears it to solitudes, erects a pyre,
And, soon as it is wasted by the fire,
Grides with disdainful claw the ashes clean ;
Then spreading unencumbered wings serene,
Mounts to the æther with renewed desire :
So joyously I lift myself above
The life I buried in hot flames to-day ;
The flames themselves are dead : and I can range
Alone through the untarnished sky I love,
And trust myself, as from the grave one may,
To the enchanting miracles of change.

PAN ASLEEP

He half unearthed the Titans with his voice,
The stars are leaves before his windy riot ;
The spheres a little shake ; but see, of choice,
How closely he wraps up in hazel quiet.
And while he sleeps the bees are numbering
The fox-glove flowers from base to sealèd tip
Till fond, they doze upon his slumbering,
And smear with honey his wide, smiling lip.
He may not be disturbed : it is the hour
That to his deepest solitude belongs ;
The unfrighted reed opens to noontide flower,
And poets hear him sing their lyric songs,
While the Arcadian hunter, baffled, hot,
Scourges his statue in its ivy-grot.

UNDER the sun on the gray hill,
  At breakfast campt behind the hedge,
  There ate he, there eats he still
Bread and bacon on the knife's edge.
  Blow the wind chill, be sky of lead,
  Or let the sun burn o'er the ridge,
Or be the cloudy fleeces spread,
  Or let rain drive, or snow come dry
  What time the blackthorn flower is shed
Like puffs of smoke on the blue sky—
  There sits he now as he sat then
  And watches how the year goes by,
And sees the world God made for men
  As little for them as it was
  In those old days of Cæsar's when
Lord Christ came riding on an ass,
  Borrowed from out some friendly stall,
  Or lifted from the common grass
And set to this new festival.
  So then to work, with heavy foot,
  To rouse his horses with a call;
And slow as they he puts them to 't,
  To hail the plow on the stony down
  Thro' marl and flint, thro' stock and root,
Where the rooks cloud the strip of brown
  And querulous peewits wheel and flock:
  Behold them on the sky-line thrown
Like giant shapes of riven rock,
  He and his team on the world's rim
  Creeping like the hands of a clock.
Or in wet meadows plashy and dim
  When winter winds blow shrill and keen,
  See him bank up the warp and swim
The eddying water over the green;
  Or follow up the hill the sheep

To where the kestrels soar and lean,
And from her form the hare doth leap
  Quick and short, and lightly flies
  Before him up the grassy steep
Where cloakt and crookt he climbs. His eyes,
  Seeing all things, and seeking none,
  Are very patient and weather-wise.
The clearest eyesight under the sun
  He has, and holds the ancient way,
  The way his forefathers have gone,
And deems himself as wise as they.

THE CHERRY-BLOSSOM WAND   *Anna Wickham*

(*To be sung.*)

I WILL pluck from my tree a cherry-blossom wand,
And carry it in my merciless hand,
So I will drive you, so bewitch your eyes,
With a beautiful thing that can never grow wise.

Light are the petals that fall from the bough,
And lighter the love that I offer you now ;
In a spring day shall the tale be told
Of the beautiful things that will never grow old.

The blossoms shall fall in the night wind,
And I will leave you so, to be kind :
Eternal in beauty are short-lived flowers,
Eternal in beauty, these exquisite hours.

I will pluck from my tree a cherry-blossom wand,
And carry it in my merciless hand,
So I will drive you, so bewitch your eyes,
With a beautiful thing that shall never grow wise.

75

FELIX RANDAL   *Gerard Manley Hopkins*

Felix Randal, the farrier, O he is dead then ? my duty
    all ended,
Who have watched his mould of man, big-boned and
    hardy-handsome
Pining, pining, till time when reason rambled in it and
    some
Fatal four disorders, fleshed there, all contended ?

Sickness broke him. Impatient he cursed at first, but
    mended
Being anointed and all ; though a heavenlier heart began
    some
Months earlier, since I had our sweet reprieve and
    ransom
Tendered to him. Ah well, God rest him all road ever
    he offended !

This seeing the sick endears them to us, us too it endears.
My tongue had taught thee comfort, touch had quenched
    thy tears,
Thy tears that touched my heart, child, Felix, poor Felix
    Randal ;

How far from then forethought of, all thy more boisterous
    years,
When thou at the random grim forge, powerful amidst
    peers,
Didst fettle for the great grey drayhorse his bright and
    battering sandal !

To Meath of the pastures,
From wet hills by the sea,
Through Leitrim and Longford,
Go my cattle and me.

I hear in the darkness
Their slipping and breathing—
I name them the bye-ways
They're to pass without heeding;

Then the wet, winding roads,
Brown bogs with black water;
And my thoughts on white ships
And the King o' Spain's daughter.

O! farmer, strong farmer!
You can spend at the fair;
But your face you must turn
To your crops and your care.

And soldiers—red soldiers!
You've seen many lands;
But you walk two by two,
And by captain's commands.

O! the smell of the beasts,
The wet wind in the morn;
And the proud and hard earth
Never broken for corn;

And the crowds at the fair,
The herds loosened and blind,
Loud words and dark faces
And the wild blood behind.

(O ! strong men, with your best
I would strive breast to breast,
I could quiet your herds
With my words, with my words.)

I will bring you, my kine,
Where there's grass to the knee ;
But you'll think of scant croppings
Harsh with salt of the sea.

PROMETHEUS   *Wilfrid Gibson*

ALL day beneath the bleak indifferent skies,
Broken and blind, a shivering bag of bones,
He trudges over icy paving-stones
And *Matches ! Matches ! Matches ! Matches !* cries.

And now beneath the dismal dripping night
And shadowed by a deeper night he stands—
And yet he holds within his palsied hands
Quick fire enough to set his world alight.

WHO ?   *Walter de la Mare*

1ST STRANGER.   Who walks with us on the hills ?
2ND STRANGER.   I cannot see for the mist.
3RD STRANGER.   Running water I hear,
                 Keeping lugubrious tryst
                 With its cresses and grasses and weeds,
                 In the white obscure light from the sky.
2ND STRANGER.   *Who walks with us on the hills ?*
WILD BIRD.   Ay ! . . . Aye ! . . . *Ay !* . . .

> Lean out of the window,
>   Goldenhair,
> I heard you singing
>   A merry air.
>
> My book is closed ;
>   I read no more,
> Watching the fire dance
>   On the floor.
>
> I have left my book :
>   I have left my room :
> For I heard you singing
>   Through the gloom,
>
> Singing and singing
>   A merry air.
> Lean out of the window,
>   Goldenhair.

Δώρια   **Ezra Pound**

> Be in me as the eternal moods
>   of the bleak wind, and not
> As transient things are—
>   gaiety of flowers.
> Have me in the strong loneliness
>   of sunless cliffs
> And of grey waters.
>   Let the gods speak softly of us
> In days hereafter,
>   The shadowy flowers of Orcus
> Remember thee.

79

THE FISHERMAN

W. B. Yeats

ALTHOUGH I can see him still
The freckled man who goes
To a grey place on a hill
In grey Connemara clothes
At dawn to cast his flies,
It's long since I began
To call up to the eyes
This wise and simple man.
All day I'd looked in the face
What I had hoped 'twould be
To write for my own race
And the reality ;
The living men that I hate,
The dead man that I loved,
The craven man in his seat,
The insolent unreproved
And no knave brought to book
Who has won a drunken cheer,
The witty man and his joke
Aimed at the commonest ear,
The clever man who cries
The catch-cries of the clown,
The beating down of the wise
And great Art beaten down.
Maybe a twelvemonth since
Suddenly I began,
In scorn of this audience
Imagining a man,
And his sun-freckled face,
And grey Connemara cloth,
Climbing up to a place
Where stone is dark under froth,
And the down turn of his wrist
When the flies drop in the stream ;
A man who does not exist,

A man who is but a dream ;
And cried, " Before I am old
I shall have written him one
Poem maybe as cold
And passionate as the dawn."

THE FURROW AND THE HEARTH (I)

Padraic Colum

STRIDE the hill, sower,
Up to the sky-ridge,
Flinging the seed,
Scattering, exultant !
Mouthing great rhythms
To the long sea beats
On the wide shore, behind
The ridge of the hillside.

Below in the darkness—
The slumber of mothers—
The cradles at rest—
The fire-seed sleeping
Deep in white ashes !

Give to darkness and sleep :
O sower, O seer !
Give me to the Earth.
With the seed I would enter.
O ! the growth thro' the silence
From strength to new strength ;
Then the strong bursting forth
Against primal forces,
To laugh in the sunshine,
To gladden the world !

THE GARDEN IN SEPTEMBER   *Robert Bridges*

Now thin mists temper the slow-ripening beams
Of the September sun : his golden gleams
On gaudy flowers shine, that prank the rows
Of high-grown hollyhocks, and all tall shows
That Autumn flaunteth in his bushy bowers ;
Where tomtits, hanging from the drooping heads
Of giant sunflowers, peck the nutty seeds ;
And in the feathery aster bees on wing
Seize and set free the honied flowers,
Till thousand stars leap with their visiting :
While ever across the path mazily flit,
Unpiloted in the sun,
The dreamy butterflies
With dazzling colours powdered and soft glooms,
White, black and crimson stripes, and peacock eyes,
Or on chance flowers sit,
With idle effort plundering one by one
The nectaries of deepest-throated blooms.

With gentle flaws the western breeze
Into the garden saileth,
Scarce here and there stirring the single trees,
For his sharpness he vaileth :
So long a comrade of the bearded corn,
Now from the stubbles whence the shocks are borne,
O'er dewy lawns he turns to stray,
As mindful of the kisses and soft play
Wherewith he enamoured the light-hearted May,
Ere he deserted her ;
Lover of fragrance, and too late repents ;
Nor more of heavy hyacinth now may drink,
Nor spicy pink,
Nor summer's rose, nor garnered lavender,
But the few lingering scents

Of streakèd pea, and gillyflower, and stocks
Of courtly purple, and aromatic phlox.

And at all times to hear are drowsy tones
Of dizzy flies, and humming drones,
With sudden flap of pigeon wings in the sky,
Or the wild cry
Of thirsty rooks, that scour ascare
The distant blue, to watering as they fare
With creaking pinions, or—on business bent,
If aught their ancient polity displease,—
Come gathering to their colony, and there
Settling in ragged parliament,
Some stormy council hold in the high trees.

A PEASANT WOMAN   *Frances Cornford*

I SAW you sit waiting with your sewing on your knees,
Till a man should claim the comfort of your body
And your industry and presence for his own.

I saw you sit waiting with your sewing on your knees,
Till the child growing hidden in your body
Should become a living creature in the light.

I saw you sit waiting with your sewing on your knees;
Till your child who had ventured to the city
Should return to the shelter of his home.

I saw you sit waiting with your sewing on your knees
—Your unreturning son was in the city—
Till Death should come along the cobbled street.

I saw you sit waiting with your sewing on your knees.

WE have bit no forbidden apple,
    Eve and I,
Yet the splashes of day and night
Falling round us, no longer dapple
The same valley with purple and white

This is our own still valley,
    Our Eden, our home ;
But day shows it vivid with feeling,
And the pallor of night does not tally
With dark sleep that once covered the ceiling,

The little red heifer : to-night I looked in her eyes ;
    She will calve to-morrow.
Last night, when I went with the lantern, the sow was
    grabbing her litter
With snarling red jaws ; and I heard the cries
Of the new-born, and then, the old owl, then the bats
    that flitter.

And I woke to the sound of the wood-pigeon, and lay
    and listened
    Till I could borrow
A few quick beats from a wood-pigeon's heart ; and
    when I did rise
Saw where morning sun on the shaken iris glistened.
And I knew that home, this valley, was wider than
    Paradise.

I learned it all from Eve,
    The warm, dumb wisdom ;
She's a quicker instructress than years ;
She has quickened my pulse to receive
Strange throbs, beyond laughter and tears.

So now I know the valley
    Fleshed all like me
With feelings that change and quiver
And clash, and yet seem to tally,
Like all the clash of a river
    Moves on to the sea.

THE SONG OF HONOUR
Ralph Hodgson

I CLIMBED a hill as light fell short,
And rooks came home in scramble sort,
And filled the trees and flapped and fought
And sang themselves to sleep ;
An owl from nowhere with no sound
Swung by and soon was nowhere found,
I heard him calling half-way round,
Holloing loud and deep ;
A pair of stars, faint pins of light,
Then many a star, sailed into sight,
And all the stars, the flower of night,
Were round me at a leap ;
To tell how still the valleys lay
I heard a watchdog miles away,
And bells of distant sheep.

I heard no more of bird or bell,
The mastiff in a slumber fell,
I stared into the sky,
As wondering men have always done
Since beauty and the stars were one
Though none so hard as I.

It seemed, so still the valleys were,
As if the whole world knelt at prayer,
Save me and me alone ;
So pure and wide that silence was
I feared to bend a blade of grass,
And there I stood like stone.

There, sharp and sudden, there I heard—
Ah! some wild lovesick singing bird
Woke singing in the trees?
The nightingale and babble-wren
Were in the English greenwood then,
And you heard one of these?

The babble-wren and nightingale
Sang in the Abyssinian vale
That season of the year!
Yet, true enough, I heard them plain,
I heard them both again, again,
As sharp and sweet and clear
As if the Abyssinian tree
Had thrust a bough across the sea,
Had thrust a bough across to me
With music for my ear!

I heard them both, and oh! I heard
The song of every singing bird
That sings beneath the sky,
And with the song of lark and wren
The song of mountains, moths and men
And seas and rainbows vie!

I heard the universal choir,
The Sons of Light exalt their Sire
With universal song,
Earth's lowliest and loudest notes,
Her million times ten million throats
Exalt Him loud and long,
And lips and lungs and tongues of Grace
From every part and every place
Within the shining of His face,
The Universal throng.

I heard the hymn of being sound
From every well of honour found
In human sense and soul :
The song of poets when they write
The testament of Beautysprite
Upon a flying scroll,
The song of painters when they take
A burning brush for Beauty's sake
And limn her features whole—

The song of men divinely wise
Who look and see in starry skies
Not stars so much as robins' eyes,
And when these pale away
Hear flocks of shiny pleiades
Among the plums and apple trees
Sing in the summer day—

The song of all both high and low
To some blest vision true,
The song of beggars when they throw
The crust of pity all men owe
To hungry sparrows in the snow,
Old beggars hungry too—
The song of kings of kingdoms when
They rise above their fortune Men,
And crown themselves anew—

The song of courage, heart and will
And gladness in a fight,
Of men who face a hopeless hill
With sparking and delight,
The bells and bells of song that ring
Round banners of a cause or king
From armies bleeding white—

The song of sailors every one
When monstrous tide and tempest run
At ships like bulls at red,
When stately ships are twirled and spun
Like whipping tops and help there's none
And mighty ships ten thousand ton
Go down like lumps of lead—

And song of fighters stern as they
At odds with fortune night and day,
Crammed up in cities grim and grey
As thick as bees in hives,
Hosannas of a lowly throng
Who sing unconscious of their song,
Whose lips are in their lives—

And song of some at holy war
With spells and ghouls more dread by far
Than deadly seas and cities are
Or hordes of quarrelling kings—
The song of fighters great and small
The song of pretty fighters all
And high heroic things—

The song of lovers—who knows how
Twitched up from place and time
Upon a sigh, a blush, a vow,
A curve or hue of cheek or brow,
Borne up and off from here and now
Into the void sublime !

And crying loves and passions still
In every key from soft to shrill
And numbers never done,
Dog-loyalties to faith and friend,
And loves like Ruth's of old no end,
And intermission none—

And burst on burst for beauty and
For numbers not behind,
From men whose love of motherland
Is like a dog's for one dear hand,
Sole, selfless, boundless, blind—
And song of some with hearts beside
For men and sorrows far and wide,
Who watch the world with pity and pride
And warm to all mankind—

And endless joyous music rise
From children at their play,
And endless soaring lullabies
From happy, happy mothers' eyes,
And answering crows and baby-cries,
How many who shall say!
And many a song as wondrous well
With pangs and sweets intolerable
From lonely hearths too grey to tell,
God knows how utter grey!
And song from many a house of care
When pain has forced a footing there
And there's a Darkness on the stair
Will not be turned away—

And song—that song whose singers come
With old kind tales of pity from
The Great Compassion's lips,
That make the bells of Heaven to peal
Round pillows frosty with the feel
Of Death's cold finger tips—

The song of men all sorts and kinds,
As many tempers, moods and minds
As leaves are on a tree,
As many faiths and castes and creeds,
As many human bloods and breeds
As in the world may be;

89

The song of each and all who gaze
On Beauty in her naked blaze,
Or see her dimly in a haze,
Or get her light in fitful rays
And tiniest needles even,
The song of all not wholly dark,
Not wholly sunk in stupor stark
Too deep for groping Heaven—

And alleluias sweet and clear
And wild with beauty men mishear,
From choirs of song as near and dear
To Paradise as they,
The everlasting pipe and flute
Of wind and sea and bird and brute,
And lips deaf men imagine mute
In wood and stone and clay:

The music of a lion strong
That shakes a hill a whole night long,
A hill as loud as he,
The twitter of a mouse among
Melodious greenery,
The ruby's and the rainbow's song,
The nightingale's—all three,
The song of life that wells and flows
From every leopard, lark and rose
And everything that gleams or goes
Lack-lustre in the sea.

I heard it all, each, every note
Of every lung and tongue and throat,
Ay, every rhythm and rhyme
Of everything that lives and loves
And upward, ever upward moves
From lowly to sublime!

Earth's multitudinous Sons of Light,
I heard them lift their lyric might
With each and every chanting sprite
That lit the sky that wondrous night
As far as eye could climb ?

I heard it all, I heard the whole
Harmonious hymn of being roll
Up through the chapel of my soul
And at the altar die,
And in the awful quiet then
Myself I heard, Amen, Amen,
Amen I heard me cry !
I heard it all and then although
I caught my flying senses, Oh,
A dizzy man was I !
I stood and stared ; the sky was lit,
The sky was stars all over it,
I stood, I knew not why,
Without a wish, without a will,
I stood upon that silent hill
And stared into the sky until
My eyes were blind with stars and still
I stared into the sky.

AUTUMN

T. E. Hulme

A TOUCH of cold in the Autumn night—
I walked abroad,
And saw the ruddy moon lean over a hedge
Like a red-faced farmer.
I did not stop to speak, but nodded,
And round about were the wistful stars
With white faces like town children.

WOULD I might lie like this, without the pain,
　For seven years—as one with snowy hair,
Who in the high tower dreams his dying reign—

　Lie here and watch the walls—how grey and bare,
The metal bed-post, the uncoloured screen,
　The mat, the jug, the cupboard, and the chair;

And served by an old woman, calm and clean,
　Her misted face familiar, yet unknown,
Who comes in silence, and departs unseen,

　And with no other visit, lie alone,
Nor stir, except I had my food to find
　In that dull bowl Diogenes might own.

And down my window I would draw the blind,
　And never look without, but, waiting, hear
A noise of rain, a whistling of the wind,

　And only know that flame-foot Spring is near
By trilling birds, or by the patch of sun
　Crouching behind my curtain. So, in fear,

Noon-dreams should enter, softly, one by one,
　And throng about the floor, and float and play
And flicker on the screen, while minutes run—

　The last majestic minutes of the day—
And with the mystic shadows, Shadow grow,
　Then the grey square of wall should fade away,

And glow again, and open, and disclose
　The shimmering lake in which the planets swim,
And all that lake a dewdrop on a rose.

THE SALE OF ST. THOMAS (EXTRACT)

Lascelles Abercrombie

MEN there have been who could so grimly look
That soldiers' hearts went out like candle flames
Before their eyes, and the blood perisht in them.—
But I—could I do that ? Would I not feel
The power in me if 'twas there ? And yet
'Twere a child's game to what I have to do,
For days and days with sleepless faith oppress
And terrorise the demon sea. I think
A man might, as I saw my Master once,
Pass unharmed through a storm of men, yet fail
At this that lies before me : men are mind,
And mind can conquer mind ; but how can it quell
The unappointed purpose of great waters ?—
Well, say the sea is past : why, then, I have
My feet but on the threshold of my task,
To gospel India,—my single heart
To seize into the order of its beat
All the strange blood of India, my brain
To lord the dark thought of that tann'd mankind !—
O, horrible those sweltry places are,
Where the sun comes so close, it makes the earth
Burn in a frenzy of breeding,—smoke and flame
Of lives burning up from agoniz'd loam !
Those monstrous sappy jungles of clutcht growth,
Enormous weed hugging enormous weed,
What can such fearful increase have to do
With prospering bounty ? A rage works in the ground,
Incurably, like frantic lechery,
Pouring its passion out in crops and spawns.
'Tis as the might spirit of life, that here
Walketh beautifully praising, glad of God,
Should, stepping on the poison'd Indian shore,
Breathing the Indian air of fire and steams,
Fling herself into a craze of hideous dancing,

93

The green gown whipping her swift limbs, all her body
Writhen to speak inutterable desire,
Tormented by a glee of hating God.
Nay, it must be, to visit India,
That frantic pomp and hurrying forth of life,
As if a man should enter at unawares
The dreaming mind of Satan, gorgeously
Imagining his eternal hell of lust.—
    They say the land is full of apes, which have
Their own gods and worship : how ghastly, this !—
That demons (for it must be so) should build,
In mockery of man's upward faith, the souls
Of monkeys, those lewd mammets of mankind,
Into a dreadful farce of adoration !
And flies ! a land of flies ! where the hot soil
Foul with ceaseless decay steams into flies !
So thick they pile themselves in the air above
Their meal of filth, they seem like breathing heaps
Of formless life mounded upon the earth ;
And buzzing always like the pipes and strings
Of solemn music made for sorcerers.—
I abhor flies,—to see them stare upon me
Out of their little faces of gibbous eyes ;
To feel the dry cool skin of their bodies alight
Perching upon my lips !—O yea, a dream,
A dream of impious obscene Satan, this
Monstrous frenzy of life, the Indian being !
And there are men in the dream ! What men are they ?
I've heard, naught relishes their brains so much
As to tie down a man and tease his flesh
Infamously, until a hundred pains
Hound the desiring life out of his body,
Filling his nerves with such a fearful zest
That the soul overstrained shatters beneath it,
Must I preach God to these murderous hearts ?

WHY hast thou nothing in thy face ?
Thou idol of the human race,
Thou tyrant of the human heart,
The flower of lovely youth that art ;
Yea, and that standest in thy youth
An image of eternal Truth,
With thy exuberant flesh so fair,
That only Pheidias might compare,
Ere from his chaste marmoreal form
Time had decayed the colours warm :
Like to his gods in thy proud dress,
Thy starry sheen of nakedness.

Surely thy body is thy mind,
For in thy face is nought to find,
Only thy soft unchristen'd smile,
That shadows neither love nor guile,
But shameless will and power immense,
In secret sensuous innocence.

O king of joy, what is thy thought ?
I dream thou knowest it is nought,
And wouldst in darkness come, but thou
Makest the light where'er thou go.
Ah yet no victim of thy grace,
None who e'er long'd for thy embrace,
Hath cared to look upon thy face.

NAPOLEON   *Walter de la Mare*

' WHAT is the world, O soldiers ?
     It is I :
I, this incessant snow,
   This northern sky ;
Soldiers, this solitude
   Through which we go
     Is I.'

God ! What a mockery is this life of ours !
Cast forth in blood and pain from our mother's womb,
Most like an excrement, and weeping showers
Of senseless tears : unreasoning, naked, dumb,
The symbol of all weakness and the sum :
Our very life a sufferance.—Presently,
Grown stronger, we must fight for standing-room
Upon the earth, and the bare liberty
To breathe and move. We crave the right to toil.
We push, we strive, we jostle with the rest.
We learn new courage, stifle our old fears,
Stand with stiff backs, take part in every broil.
It may be that we love, that we are blest.
It may be, for a little space of years,
We conquer fate and half forget our tears.

THE MOCKERY OF LIFE (II)

And then fate strikes us. First our joys decay.
Youth, with its pleasures, is a tale soon told.
We grow a little poorer day by day.
Old friendships falter. Loves grow strangely cold.
In vain we shift our hearts to a new hold
And barter joy for joy, the less for less.
We doubt our strength, our wisdom, and our gold.
We stand alone, as in a wilderness
Of doubts and terrors. Then, if we be wise,
We make our terms with fate and, while we may,
Sell our life's last sad remnant for a hope.
And it is wisdom thus to close our eyes.
But for the foolish, those who cannot pray,
What else remains of their dark horoscope
But a tall tree and courage and a rope ?

THE MOCKERY OF LIFE (III)

AND who shall tell what ignominy death
Has yet in store for us ; what abject fears
Even for the best of us ; what fights for breath ;
What sobs, what supplications, what wild tears ;
What impotence of soul against despairs
Which blot out reason ?—The last trembling thought
Of each poor brain, as dissolution nears,
Is not of fair life lost, of Heaven bought
And glory won. 'Tis not the thought of grief ;
Of friends deserted ; loving hearts which bleed ;
Wives, sisters, children who around us weep.
But only a mad clutching for relief
From physical pain, importunate Nature's need ;
The search as for a womb where we may creep
Back from the world, to hide,—perhaps to sleep.

THE TWO HIGHWAYMEN

I LONG have had a quarrel set with Time,
Because he robbed me. Every day of life
Was wrested from me after bitter strife,
I never yet could see the sun go down
But I was angry in my heart, nor hear
The leaves fall in the wind without a tear
Over the dying summer. I have known
No truce with Time, nor, Time's accomplice, Death.
The fair world is the witness of a crime
Repeated every hour. For life and breath
Are sweet to all who live ; and bitterly
The voices of these robbers of the heath
Sound in each ear and chill the passer by.
What have we done to thee, thou monstrous Time ?
What have we done to Death that we must die ?

THE FRESH START

Anna Wickham

O GIVE me back my rigorous English Sunday
And my well-ordered house, with stockings washed on
    Monday.
Let the House-Lord, that kindly decorous fellow,
Leave happy for his Law at ten, with a well-furled
    umbrella.
Let my young sons observe my strict house rules,
Imbibing Tory principles, at Tory schools.

Two years now I have sat beneath a curse
And in a fury poured out frenzied verse.
Such verse as held no beauty and no good
And was at best new curious vermin-food.

My dog is rabid, and my cat is lean,
And not a pot in all this place is clean.
The locks have fallen from my hingeless doors,
And holes are in my credit and my floors.

There is no solace for me, but in sooth
To have said baldly certain ugly truth.
Such scavenger's work was never yet a woman's,
My wardrobe's more a scarecrow's than a human's.

I'm off to the House-goddess for her gift.
" O give me Circumspection, Temperance, Thrift ;
Take thou this lust of words, this fevered itching,
And give me faith in darning, joy of stitching ! "

When this hot blood is cooled by kindly Time
Controlled and schooled, I'll come again to Rhyme.
Sure of my methods, morals and my gloves,
I'll write chaste sonnets of imagined Loves.

THE TIRED MAN

I AM a quiet gentleman,
And I would sit and dream ;
But my wife is on the hillside,
Wild as a hill-stream.

I am a quiet gentleman,
And I would sit and think ;
But my wife is walking the whirlwind
Through night as black as ink.

O, give me a woman of my race
As well controlled as I,
And let us sit by the fire,
Patient till we die !

SOUL'S LIBERTY

HE who has lost soul's liberty
Concerns himself for ever with his property,
As, when the folk have lost both dance and song,
Women clean useless pots the whole day long.

Thank God for war and fire
To burn the silly objects of desire,
That from the ruin of a church thrown down
We see God clear and high above the town.

AFTER ANNUNCIATION

REST, little Guest,
Beneath my breast.
Feed, sweet Seed,
At your need.
I took Love for my lord
And this is my reward,
My body is good earth,
That you, dear Plant, have birth.

FIVE-AND-TWENTY years have gone
Since old William Pollexfen
Laid his strong bones down in death
By his wife Elizabeth
In the grey stone tomb he made.
And after twenty years they laid
In that tomb by him and her,
His son George, the astrologer ;
And Masons drove from miles away
To scatter the Acacia spray
Upon a melancholy man
Who had ended where his breath began.
Many a son and daughter lies
Far from the customary skies,
The Mall and Eades's grammar school,
In London or in Liverpool ;
But where is laid the sailor John ?
That so many lands had known :
Quiet lands or unquiet seas
Where the Indians trade or Japanese.
He never found his rest ashore
Moping for one voyage more.
Where have they laid the sailor John ?
And yesterday the youngest son,
A humorous, unambitious man,
Was buried near the astrologer ;
And are we now in the tenth year ?
Since he, who had been contented long,
A nobody in a great throng,
Decided he would journey home,
Now that his fiftieth year had come,
And " Mr Alfred " be again
Upon the lips of common men
Who carried in their memory
His childhood and his family.

At all these death-beds women heard
A visionary white sea-bird
Lamenting that a man should die ;
And with that cry I have raised my cry.

THE YOUNG CORN IN CHORUS   *T. Sturge Moore*

ALL we, the young corn, stalwart stand
In millions upright side by side,
And countless acres of the land
In orderly close chorus hide,
Shouting : " Gold, of his largess,
And health he discharges
Both far and wide ! "

Though all the world were brimmed with gold
And valleys with health had over-run,
Who could command his hand to hold,
Contest the giving of the sun ?
Hail him ; vigour for growing
He cometh bestowing
On each weak one !

The winds, with showers on their backs,
His servants, lounge by distant seas ;
And far-seen summits of their packs
Heave up when shifted for their ease,—
Wearied long there attending
Lest heat of his sending
Cloy those he would please.

BABEL: THE GATE OF THE GOD *Gordon Bottomley*

Lost towers impend, copeless primeval props
Of the new threatening sky, and first rude digits
Of awe, remonstrance and uneasy power
Thrust out by man when speech sank back in his throat:
Then had the last rocks ended bubbling up
And rhythms of change within the heart begun
By a blind need that would make Springs and Winters;
Pylons and monoliths went on by ages,
Mycenae and Great Zimbabwe came about;
Cowed hearts in This conceived a pyramid
That leaned to hold itself upright, a thing
Foredoomed to limits, death and an easy apex;
Then postulants for the stars' previous wisdom
Standing on Carthage must get nearer still;
While in Chaldea an altitude of god
Being mooted, and a saurian unearthed
Upon a mountain stirring a surmise
Of floods and alterations of the sea,
A round-walled tower must rise upon Senaar
Temple and escape to god the ascertained.
These are decayed like Time's teeth in his mouth,
Black cavities and gaps, yet earth is darkened
By their deep-sunken and unfounded shadows
And memories of man's earliest theme of towers.

Space—the old source of time—should be undone,
Eternity defined, by men who trusted
Another tier would equal them with god.
A city of grimy kilns and monstrous vats
Of walled-in metal where thick bitumen
Boiled to make grout and mortar and exhaled
Itself in sooty vapour, squat truncations,
Hunched like spread toads yet beetled under their circles
Of low packed smoke, assemblages of thunder

That glowed upon their under sides by night
And lit like storm small shadowless workmen's toil.
Meaningless stumps, upturned bare roots, remained
In fields of mashy mud and trampled leaves ;
While, if a horse died hauling, plasterers
Knelt on a flank to clip its sweaty coat.

A builder leans across the last wide courses ;
His unadjustable unreaching eyes
Fail under him before his glances sink
On the clouds' upper layers of sooty curls
Where some long lightning goes like swallows downward,
But at the wider gallery next below
Recognize master-masons with pricked parchments :
That builder then, as one who condescends
Unto the sea and all that is beneath him,
His hairy breast on the wet mortar, calls
" How many fathoms is it yet to heaven ! "
On the next eminence the orgulous king
Nimroud stands up conceiving he shall live
To conquer god, now that he knows where god is :
His eager hands push up the tower in thought . . .
Again, his shaggy inhuman height strides down
Among the carpenters because he has seen
One shape an eagle-woman on a door-post :
He drives his spear-beam through him for wasted day.

Little men hurrying, running here and there,
Within the dark and stifling walls, dissent
From every sound, and shoulder empty hods :
" The god's great altar should stand in the crypt
Among our earth's foundations "—" The god's great
     altar
Must be the last far coping of our work "—

" It should inaugurate the broad main stair "—
" Or end it "—" It must stand toward the East ! "
But here a grave contemptuous youth cries out
" Womanish babblers, how can we build god's altar
Ere we divine its foreordained true shape ? "
Then one " It is a pedestal for deeds "—
" 'Tis more and should be hewn like the king's brow "—
" It has the nature of a woman's bosom "—
" The tortoise, first created, signifies it "—
" A blind and rudimentary navel shows
The source of worship better than horned moons."
Then a lean giant " Is not a calyx needful ? "—
" Because round grapes on statues well expressed
Become the nadir of incense, nodal lamps,
Yet apes have hands thad but and carved red crystal "—
" Birds molten, touchly talc veins bronze buds crumble
Ablid ublai ghan isz rad eighar ghaurl. . . . "
Words said too often seemed such ancient sounds
That men forgot them or were lost in them ;
The guttural glottis-chasms of language reached,
A rhythm, a gasp, were curves of immortal thought.

Man with his bricks was building, building yet,
Where dawn and midnight mingled and woke no birds,
In the last courses, building past his knowledge
A wall that swung—for towers can have no tops,
No chord can mete the universal segment,
Earth has not basis. Yet the yielding sky,
Invincible vacancy, was there discovered—
Though piled-up bricks should pulp the sappy balks,
Weight generate a secrecy of heat,
Cankerous charring, crevices' fronds of flame.

SHELLEY'S SKYLARK *Thomas Hardy*

SOMEWHERE afield here something lies
In Earth's oblivious eyeless trust
That moved a poet to prophecies—
A pinch of unseen, unguarded dust :

The dust of the lark that Shelley heard,
And made immortal through times to be ;—
Though it only lived like another bird,
And knew not its immortality :

Lived its meek life ; then, one day, fell—
A little ball of feather and bone ;
And how it perished, when piped farewell,
And where it wastes, are alike unknown.

Maybe it rests in the loam I view,
Maybe it throbs in a myrtle's green,
Maybe it sleeps in the coming hue
Of a grape on the slopes of yon inland scene.

Go find it, faeries, go and find
That tiny pinch of priceless dust,
And bring a casket silver-lined,
And framed of gold that gems encrust ;

And we will lay it safe therein,
And consecrate it to endless time ;
For it inspired a bard to win
Ecstatic heights in thought and rhyme.

THE FUNERAL OF YOUTH: THRENODY

Rupert Brooke

THE day that *Youth* had died,
There came to his grave-side,
In decent mourning, from the county's ends,
Those scatter'd friends
Who had liv'd the boon companions of his prime,
And laugh'd with him and sung with him and wasted,
In feast and wine and many crown'd carouse,
The days and nights and dawnings of the time
When *Youth* kept open house,
Nor left untasted
Aught of his high emprise and ventures dear,
No quest of his unshar'd—
All these, with loitering feet and sad head bar'd,
Follow'd their old friend's bier.
Folly went first,
With muffled bells and coxcomb still revers'd ;
And after trod the bearers, hat in hand—
Laughter, most hoarse, and Captain *Pride* with tann'd
And martial face all grim, and fussy *Joy*,
Who had to catch a train, and *Lust*, poor, snivelling boy ;
These bore the dear departed.
Behind them, broken-hearted,
Came *Grief*, so noisy a widow, that all said,
' Had he but wed
Her elder sister *Sorrow*, in her stead ! '
And by her, trying to soothe her all the time,
The fatherless children, *Colour*, *Tune*, and *Rhyme*
(The sweet lad *Rhyme*), ran all-uncomprehending.
Then, at the way's sad ending,
Round the raw grave they stay'd. Old *Wisdom* read,
In mumbling tone, the Service for the Dead.
There stood *Romance*,
The furrowing tears had mark'd her rougèd cheek ;
Poor old *Conceit*, his wonder unassuag'd ;
Dead *Innocency's* daughter, *Ignorance* ;

And shabby, ill-dress'd *Generosity*;
And *Argument*, too full of woe to speak;
Passion, grown portly, something middle-aged;
And *Friendship*—not a minute older, she;
Impatience, ever taking out his watch;
Faith, who was deaf, and had to lean, to catch
Old *Wisdom's* endless drone.
Beauty was there,
Pale in her black; dry-ey'd; she stood alone.
Poor maz'd *Imagination*; *Fancy* wild;
Ardour, the sunlight on his greying hair;
Contentment, who had known *Youth* as a child
And never seen him since. And *Spring* came too,
Dancing over the tombs, and brought him flowers—
She did not stay for long.
And *Truth*, and *Grace*, and all the merry crew,
The laughing *Winds* and *Rivers*, and lithe *Hours*;
And *Hope*, the dewy-ey'd; and sorrowing *Song*;—
Yes, with much woe and mourning general,
At dead *Youth's* funeral,
Even these were met once more together, all,
Who erst the fair and living *Youth* did know;
All, except only *Love*. *Love* had died long ago.

THE LAST JOURNEY

John Davidson

I FELT the world a-spinning on its nave,
  I felt it sheering blindly round the sun;
I felt the time had come to find a grave:
  I knew it in my heart my days were done.
I took my staff in hand; I took the road,
And wandered out to seek my last abode.
      Hearts of gold and hearts of lead
        Sing it yet in sun and rain,
          " Heel and toe from dawn to dusk,
          Round the world and home again."

O long before the bere was steeped for malt,
  And long before the grape was crushed for wine,
The glory of the march without a halt,
  The triumph of a stride like yours and mine
Was known to folk like us, who walked about,
To be the sprightliest cordial out and out!
    Folk like us, with hearts that beat,
      Sang it too in sun and rain—
      " Heel and toe from dawn to dusk,
      Round the world and home again."

My feet are heavy now, but on I go,
  My head erect beneath the tragic years.
The way is steep, but I would have it so ;
  And dusty, but I lay the dust with tears,
Though none can see me weep : alone I climb
The rugged path that leads me out of time—
    Out of time and out of all,
      Singing yet in sun and rain,
      " Heel and toe from dawn to dusk,
      Round the world and home again."

Farewell the hope that mocked, farewell despair
  That went before me still and made the pace.
The earth is full of graves, and mine was there
  Before my life began, my resting-place ;
And I shall find it out and with the dead
Lie down for ever, all my sayings said—
    Deeds all done and songs all sung,
      While others chant in sun and rain,
      " Heel and toe from dawn to dusk,
      Round the world and home again."

OLD lady, when last year I sipped your tea
And wooed you with my deference to discuss
The elegance of your embroidery,
I felt no forethought of our meeting thus.
　　Last week your age was ' almost eighty-three.'
　　To-day you own the eternal over-plus.
　　These moments are ' experience ' for me ;
　　But not for you ; not for a mutual ' us.'

I visit you unwelcomed ; you've no time
Left to employ in afternoon politeness.
You've only Heaven's great stairway now to climb,
And your long load of years has changed to lightness.
　　When Oxford belfries chime you do not hear,
　　Nor in this mellow-toned autumnal brightness
　　Observe an English-School-like atmosphere . . .
　　You have inherited everlasting whiteness.

You lived your life in grove and garden shady
Of social Academe, good talk and taste :
But now you are a very quiet old lady,
Stiff, sacrosanct, and alabaster-faced.
　　And, while I tip-toe awe-struck from your room,
　　I fail to synthesize your earth-success
　　With this, your semblance to a sculptured tomb
　　That clasps a rosary of nothingness.

I took my oath I would inquire,
  Without affection, hate, or wrath,
Into the death of Ada Wright—
  So help me God! I took that oath.

When I went out to see the corpse,
  The four months' babe that died so young,
I judged it was seven pounds in weight,
  And little more than one foot long.

One eye, that had a yellow lid,
  Was shut—so was the mouth, that smiled ;
The left eye open, shining bright—
  It seemed a knowing little child.

For as I looked at that one eye,
  It seemed to laugh, and say with glee :
' What caused my death you'll never know—
  Perhaps my mother murdered me.'

When I went into court again,
  To hear the mother's evidence—
It was a love-child, she explained.
  And smiled, for our intelligence.

' Now, Gentlemen of the Jury,' said
  The coroner—' this woman's child
By misadventure met its death.'
  ' Aye, aye,' said we. The mother smiled.

And I could see that child's one eye
  Which seemed to laugh, and say with glee :
' What caused my death you'll never know—
  Perhaps my mother murdered me.'

THE FLIGHT INTO EGYPT *Peter Quennell*

WITHIN Heaven's circle I had not guessed at this,
I had not guessed at pleasure such as this,
So sharp a pleasure,
That, like a lamp burning in foggy night,
Makes its own orb and sphere of flowing gold
And tents itself in light.

Going before you, now how many days,
Thoughts, all turned back like birds against the wind,
Wheeled sullenly towards my Father's house,
Considered his blind presence and the gathered, bustling
   pæan,
The affluence of his sweetness, his grace and unageing
   might.

My flesh glowed then in the shadow of a loose cloak
And my brightness troubled the ground with every pulse
   of the blood,
My wings lax on the air, my eyes open and grave,
With the vacant pride of hardly less than a god.

We passed thickets that quaked with hidden deer,
And wide shallows dividing before my feet,
Empty plains threaded, and between stiff aloes
I took the asse's bridle to climb into mountain pathways.

When cold bit you, through your peasant's mantle,
And my Father filled the air with meaningless stars,
I brought dung and dead white grass for fuel,
Blowing a fire with the breath of the holy word.

Your drudge, Joseph, slept; you would sit unmoving,
In marble quiet, or by the unbroken voice of a river,

Would sometimes bare your maiden breast to his mouth,
The suckling, to the conscious God balanced upon your
    knees.

Apart I considered the melodious names of my brothers,
As again in my Father's house, and the even spheres
Slowly, nightlong recalled the splendour of numbers ;
I heard again the voluptuous measure of praise.

Sometimes pacing beneath clarity immeasurable
I saw my mind lie open and desert,
The wavering streams frozen up and each coppice
    quieted,
A whole valley in starlight with leaves and waters.

Coming at last to these farthest Syrian hills,
Attis or Adon, some ambushed lust looked out ;
My skin grows pale and smooth, shrunken as silk,
Without the rough effulgence of a God.

And here no voice has spoken ;
There is no shrine of any godhead here
No grove or hallowed fires,
And godhead seems asleep.

Only the vine has woven
Strange houses and blind rooms and palaces,
Into each hollow and crevice continually
Dropped yearlong irrecoverable flowers.

The sprawling vine has built us a close room
Obedient Hymen fills the air with mist ;
And to make dumb our theft
The white and moving sand that will not bear a print.

" WHAT have you looked at, Moon,
In your time,
Now long past your prime ? "
" O, I have looked at, often looked at
Sweet, sublime,
Sore things, shudderful, night and noon
In my time."

" What have you mused on, Moon,
In your day,
So aloof, so far away ? "
" O, I have mused on, often mused on
Growth, decay,
Nations alive, dead, mad, aswoon,
In my day ! "

" Have you much wondered, Moon,
On your rounds,
Self-wrapt, beyond Earth's bounds ? "
" Yea, I have wondered, often wondered
At the sounds
Reaching me of the human tune
On my rounds."

" What do you think of it, Moon,
As you go ?
Is Life much, or no ? "
" O, I think of it, often think of it
As a show
God ought surely to shut up soon,
As I go."

THEY shall be heard to-morrow ;
  Their little flutes, their happy little flutes,
    Time shall snatch from them never ;
They that have outlived sorrow,
    Their piping is forever.

Where have their feet been straying ?
  The wanderers, the careless wanderers,
    Pray them to linger near us.
For love of their sweet playing
    They have no thought to hear us.

Where are the resting-places
  Our hearts, our hurried hearts have fashioned for them,
    That they go past so blindly ?
Scorn is not in their faces,
    Nor any look unkindly.

Of resting, what need have they ?
  Ours are the eyes that flinch from looking forward.
    Their path is hither, thither ;
And what sign ever gave they
    Of journey anywhither ?

We hear them when we tarry,
  When we rest too, from utter sorrow when
    We hide our hearts from living,
And are too worn to parry
    The weapons of misgiving.

But when with waking cometh
  The strength to rise, the strength we would not call on,
    For the desire of slumber ;
The imp of silence drummeth
    And doth our ears encumber.

If we pursue, the rather
 They flee, those sounds, they wrap them up in darkness;
  The voices of our yearning
Fly far away, and farther
  The hope of their returning.

It needs another breaking
 Of camp, another and another journey;
  Land and sea marches spending,
A world of overtaking;
  Then haply, no sweet ending.

What if forever, gaining,
 The only shore, the steep, sea-silenced country
  Of our hearts' heavy winging,
We find no voice remaining,
  Nor custom of sweet singing?

May then our hearts so heavy
 Turn back, turn out of the storm-riven mountain,
  Or shall its warders find us,
Its wild torch-bearers chevy,
  Until the darkness bind us?

And shall we never hear them,
 The voices that we know to be eternal;
  The sounds so true about us,
The flutes, and those that bear them,
  Can they play on without us?

Music, such music spending,
 And all the sounds they make the sounds that gave us
  This too sad love of being;
This too sad, too soon ending,
  Blind grasping, empty seeing?

O eyes regardless, gleaming
  Above the twinkling stops of your sweet staves ;
    And feet that tread the measure
And circuit of our dreaming :
    Yours is not all the treasure ;

On, on, and on divinely :
  Far we have wandered too and left great labours ;
    The burden of your ditties
Is of a house built finely ;
    And builders we of cities.

The little palms that twinkle
  The smooth flute length along move not too swiftly
    To cover from our gazing
The rift of many a wrinkle
    And sheath of horny hazing.

Children or old men are they ?
  Their wide eyes are alive like those, like these
    Deep-set and furrow-bearing ;
And with what rude stains mar they
    Their hues of homespun wearing ?

Their cheeks with breath are swelling,
  Their limbs, their ready feet are those of children ;
    Their wise brows bent not, lightly
Their tale of wisdom telling,
    Nor sight of it unsightly.

It must be they are older
  Than wisdom need, and have childheartedness.
    Strong, but a little stronger
Than death, and how much bolder,
    And then, to pipe the longer.

And to go on, and never
 Tire of the sweet staves of their slender pipe ;
  They that have outlived sorrow,
Whose piping is forever,
  Whose piping is to-morrow.

THE WILD ASS   *Padraic Colum*

 THE wild ass lounges, legs struck out
 In vagrom unconcern :
 The tombs of Achæmedian kings
 Are for those hooves to spurn.

 And all of rugged Tartary
 Lies with him on the ground,
 The Tartary that knows no awe,
 That has nor ban nor bound.

 The wild horse from the herd is plucked
 To bear a saddle's weight ;
 The boar is one keeps covert, and
 The wolf runs with a mate ;

 But he's the solitary of space,
 Curbless and unbeguiled ;
 The only being that bears a heart
 Not recreant to the wild.

LONG are the hours the sun is above,
But when evening comes I go home to my love.

I'm away the daylight hours and more,
Yet she comes not down to open the door.

She does not meet me upon the stair,—
She sits in my chamber and waits for me there.

As I enter the room she does not move:
I always walk straight up to my love;

And she lets me take my wonted place
At her side, and gaze in her dear dear face.

There as I sit, from her head thrown back
Her hair falls straight in a shadow black.

Aching and hot as my tired eyes be,
She is all that I wish to see.

And in my wearied and toil-dinned ear,
She says all things that I wish to hear.

Dusky and duskier grows the room,
Yet I see her best in the darker gloom.

When the winter eves are early and cold,
The firelight hours are a dream of gold.

And so I sit here night by night,
In rest and enjoyment of love's delight.

But a knock at the door, a step on the stair
Will startle, alas, my love from her chair.

If a stranger comes she will not stay:
At the first alarm she is off and away.

And he wonders, my guest, usurping her throne
That I sit so much by myself alone.

LUBBER BREEZE   *T. Sturge Moore*

THE four sails of the mill
Like stocks stand still;
Their lantern-length is white
On blue more bright.

Unruffled is the mead
Where lambkins feed,
And sheep and cattle browse,
And donkeys drowse.

Never the least breeze will
The wet thumb chill
That the anxious miller lifts,
Till the vane shifts.

The breeze in the great flour-bin
Is snug tucked in;
The lubber, while rats thieve,
Laughs in his sleeve.

F. S. Flint

THE hollow sound of your hard felt hat
As you clap it on your head
Is echoed over two thousand miles of trenches
By a thousand thousand guns ;
And thousands of thousands of men have been killed,
And still more thousands of thousands have bled
And been maimed and have drowned
Because of that sound.

Towns battered and shattered,
Villages blasted to dust and mud,
Forests and woods stripped bare,
Rivers and streams befouled,
The earth between and beyond the lines
Ravaged and sown with steel
And churned with blood
And astink with decaying men,
Nations starving, women and children murdered,
Genius destroyed, minds deformed and twisted,
And waste, waste, waste
Of the earth's fruits, of the earth's riches,—
All in obedience to your voice ;
And the sound of your hat
Is in the same gamut of void and thoughtless
And evil sounds.

O estimable man,
Keeper of the season ticket,
Walker on the pavement,
Follower of the leader writer,
Guardian of the life policy,
Insured against all harm—

Fire, burglary, servants' accidents—
Warden and ward of the church,
Wallflower of the suburbs,
Primrose of respectability,
As you go home beneath your hard felt hat
The tradesmen do you homage.
Happily, the trees do not know you.

You have scoffed at the poet,
Because you are a practical man :
And does not your house bear you out ?
Have poets such houses ?
It has a garden in front with a plot of grass,
And in the middle of that a flower-bed.
With a rose-tree in its midst, and other rose-trees
Against the walls, and a privet hedge,
And stocks and delphiniums, flowers in season !
The path is irregularly paved for quaintness ;
There is a rustic porch, and a street door
With a polished brass letter-box and knocker,
And stained glass panels, showing a bird and flowers,
And an electric-bell push.
But you have a key, and you let yourself in
To the quiet red-tiled hall, where the doormat
Says " Welcome," and the stand receives your umbrella
And your coat and your hard felt hat.
A drawing-room, a dining-room (because
All your fellows have them), and a kitchen
All clean and neat ; and because the kitchen is comfortable
You have your tea there with your wife and child—
Only one child, for are you not practical ?
On the upper floor are a bathroom and three bedrooms.
Let your furniture stand undisturbed,
I will not describe it : a hundred shops in London
Show off the like in their windows. As for your books
They are as haphazard and as futile as your pictures.

But here is your comfort and you are comfortable ;
And on summer evenings and Saturday afternoons
You wander out into the garden at the back,
Which is fenced off on three sides from similar gardens,
And you potter around with garden tools and are happy.

O insured against all harm,
Waiter on the pension at sixty,
Domestic vegetable, cultivated flower,
You have laughed at the poet, the unpractical dreamer :
You have seen life as bookkeeping and accountancy ;
Your arithmetic has pleased you, your compound interest
Your business, more than the earth and the heavens ;
And if your brother suffered, you took no heed,
Or read a liberal newspaper, and salved your conscience.
Ant, ant, oblivious of the water being boiled in the cauldron !

But when the time came for your chastisement,
For the punishment of your apathy, your will-less ignor-
ance,
When the atmospheric pressure was just equivalent
To the weight of the seventy-six centimetre column of
mercury,
And the water had exactly reached the hundredth degree
of centigrade,
You felt, though you feared it, that the time had come,
That you had something called a collective honour, some
patriotism ;
And those others too felt the same honourable sentiment,
And you called for the slaughter that sanctifies honour,
And the boiling water was poured on us all.   Ants !   Ants !

Friend and brother, you have not been killed ;
Chance still allows you to wear your bowler hat,
The helmet of the warrior in its degeneracy,
The symbol of gracelessness and of the hate of beauty,
The signature of your sameness and innocuousness.

Take off your hat ; let your hair grow ; open your eyes
Look at your neighbour ; his suffering is your hurt.
Become dangerous ; let the metaphysical beast
Whose breath poisons us all fear your understanding,
And recoil from our bodies, his prey, and fall back before
    you,
And shiver and quake and thirst and starve and die.

EAU-FORTE

On black bare trees a stale cream moon
Hangs dead, and sours the unborn buds.

Two gaunt old hacks, knees bent, heads low,
Tug, tired and spent, an old horse tram.

Damp smoke, rank mist fill the dark square ;
And round the bend six bullocks come.

A hobbling, dirt-grimed drover guides
Their clattering feet—
        their clattering feet !
          to the slaughterhouse.

THE SCENE OF WAR : FEAR   *Herbert Read*

Fear is a wave
Beating through the air
And on taut nerves impingeing
Till there it wins
Vibrating chords.

All goes well
So long as you tune the instrument
To simulate composure.

(So you will become
A gallant gentleman.)

But when the strings are broken. . . .
Then you will grovel on the earth
And your rabbit eyes
Will fill with the fragments of your shattered soul.

THE SCENE OF WAR: THE HAPPY WARRIOR

His wild heart beats with painful sobs,
His strained hands clench an ice-cold rifle,
His aching jaws grip a hot parched tongue,
And his wide eyes search unconsciously

He cannot shriek.

Bloody saliva
Dribbles down his shapeless jacket.

I saw him stab
And stab again
A well-killed Boche.

This is the happy warrior,
This is he. . . .

ON THE WINGS OF THE MORNING   *Jeffery Day*

A SUDDEN roar, a mighty rushing sound,
   a jolt or two, a smoothly sliding rise,
a jumbled blur of disappearing ground,
   and then all sense of motion slowly dies.
      Quiet and calm, the earth slips past below,
      As underneath a bridge still waters flow.

My turning wing inclines towards the ground ;
   the ground itself glides up with graceful swing
and at the plane's far tip twirls slowly round,
   then drops from sight again beneath the wing
      to slip away serenely as before,
      a cubist-patterned carpet on the floor.

Hills gently sink and valleys gently fill.
   The flattened fields grow infinitely small ;
slowly they pass beneath and slower still
   until they hardly seem to move at all.
      Then suddenly they disappear from sight,
      hidden by fleeting wisps of faded white.

The wing-tips, faint and dripping, dimly show,
   blurred by the wreaths of mist that intervene.
Weird, half-seen shadows flicker to and fro
   across the pallid fog-bank's blinding screen.
      At last the choking mists release their hold,
      and all the world is silver, blue, and gold.

The air is clear, more clear than sparkling wine ;
   compared with this, wine is a turgid brew.
The far horizon makes a clean-cut line
   between the silver and the depthless blue.
      Out of the snow-white level reared on high
      glittering hills surge up to meet the sky.

Outside the wind screen's shelter gales may race :
  but in the seat a cool and gentle breeze
blows steadily upon my grateful face
    as I sit motionless and at my ease,
      contented just to loiter in the sun
      and gaze around me till the day is done.

And so I sit, half sleeping, half awake,
  dreaming a happy dream of golden days,
until at last, with a reluctant shake,
    I rouse myself, and with a lingering gaze
      at all the splendour of the shining plain
      make ready to come down to earth again.

The engine stops : a pleasant silence reigns—
  silence, not broken, but intensified
by the soft, sleepy wires' insistent strains,
    that rise and fall, as with a sweeping glide
      I slither down the well-oiled sides of space
      towards a lower, less enchanted place.

The clouds draw nearer, changing as they come.
  Now, like a flash, fog grips me by the throat.
Down goes the nose : at once the wires' low hum
    begins to rise in volume and in note,
      till as I hurtle from the choking cloud
      it swells into a scream, high-pitched and loud.

The scattered hues and shades of green and brown
  fashion themselves into the land I know,
Turning and twisting, as I spiral down
    towards the landing-ground ; till, skimming low,
      I glide with slackening speed across the ground,
      And come to rest with lightly grating sound.

HEREDITY

I AM the family face ;
Flesh perishes, I live on,
Projecting trait and trace
Through time to times anon,
And leaping from place to place
Over oblivion.

The years-heired feature that can
In curve and voice and eye
Despise the human span
Of durance—that is I ;
The eternal thing in man,
That heeds no call to die.

TENANTS

Wilfrid Gibson

SUDDENLY out of dark and leafy ways
We came upon the little house asleep
In cold blind stillness, shadowless and deep,
In the white magic of the full moon-blaze :
Strangers without the gate we stood agaze,
Fearful to break the quiet and to creep
Into the house that had been ours to keep
Through a long year of happy nights and days.

So unfamiliar in the white moon-gleam,
So old and ghostly like a house of dream
It seemed, that over us there stole the dread
That, even as we watched it side by side,
The ghosts of lovers, who had lived and died
Within its walls, were sleeping in our bed.

127

NOT ON SAD STYGIAN SHORE   *Samuel Butler*

NOT on sad Stygian shore, nor in clear sheen
Of far Elysian plain, shall we meet those
Among the dead whose pupils we have been,
Nor those great shades whom we have held as foes ;
No meadow of asphodel our feet shall tread,
Nor shall we look each other in the face
To love or hate each other being dead,
Hoping some praise, or fearing some disgrace.
We shall not argue, saying " 'Twas thus ", or " thus "
Our argument's whole drift we shall forget ;
Who's right, who's wrong, 'twill be all one to us ;
We shall not even know that we have met.
   Yet meet we shall, and part, and meet again,
   Where dead men meet, on lips of living men.

THE HILL   *Rupert Brooke*

BREATHLESS, we flung us on the windy hill,
  Laughed in the sun, and kissed the lovely grass
  You said, ' Through glory and ecstasy we pass ;
Wind, sun, and earth remain, the birds sing still,
When we are old, are old. . . .' ' And when we die
  All's over that is ours ; and life burns on
Through other lovers, other lips ', said I,
  ' Heart of my heart, our heaven is now, is won ! '

' We are Earth's best, that learnt her lesson here.
  Life is our cry. We have kept the faith ! ' we said ;
  ' We shall go down with unreluctant tread
Rose-crowned into the darkness ! ' . . . Proud we were,
And laughed, that had such brave true things to say.
—And then you suddenly cried, and turned away.

THE LEADEN ECHO AND THE GOLDEN ECHO

(MAIDENS' SONG FROM ST. WINEFRED'S WELL)

Gerard Manley Hopkins

THE LEADEN ECHO

How to kéep—is there ány any, is there none such,
 nowhere known some, bow or brooch or braid or
 brace, láce, latch or catch or key to keep
Back beauty, keep it, beauty, beauty, beauty, . . . from
 vanishing away ?
Ó is there no frowning of these wrinkles, rankèd wrinkles
 deep,
Dówn ? no waving off of these most mournful messengers,
 still messengers, sad and stealing messengers of grey ?
No there's none, there's none, O no there's none,
Nor can you long be, what you now are, called fair,
Do what you may do, what, do what you may,
And wisdom is early to despair :
Be beginning ; since, no, nothing can be done
To keep at bay
Age and age's evils, hoar hair,
Ruck and wrinkle, drooping, dying, death's worst, winding
 sheets, tombs and worms and tumbling to decay ;
So be beginning, be beginning to despair.
O there's none ; no no no there's none :
Be beginning to despair, to despair,
Despair, despair, despair, despair.

THE GOLDEN ECHO

   Spare !
There ís one, yes I have one (Hush there !) ;
Only not within seeing of the sun,
Not within the singeing of the strong sun,
Tall sun's tingeing, or teacherous the tainting of the
 earth's air,

Somewhere elsewhere there is ah well where ! one,
One.   Yes I can tell such a key, I do know such a place,
Where whatever's prized and passes of us, everything
        that's fresh and fast flying of us, seems to us sweet of
        us and swiftly away with, done away with, undone,
Undone, done with, soon done with, and yet dearly and
        dangerously sweet
Of us, the wimpled-water-dimpled, not-by-morning-
        matchèd face,
The flower of beauty, fleece of beauty, too too apt to, ah !
        to fleet,
Never fleets móre, fastened with the tenderest truth
To its own best being and its loveliness of youth : it is
        an ever-lastingness of, O it is an all youth !
Come then, your ways and airs and looks, locks, maiden
        gear, gallantry and gaiety and grace,
Winning ways, airs innocent, maiden manners, sweet looks,
        loose locks, long locks, lovelocks, gaygear, going
        gallant, girlgrace—
Resign them, sign them, seal them, send them, motion
        them with breath,
And with sighs soaring, soaring síghs deliver
Them ; beauty-in-the-ghost, deliver it, early now, long
        before death
Give beauty back, beauty, beauty, beauty, back to God,
        beauty's self and beauty's giver.
See ; not a hair is, not an eyelash, not the least lash lost ;
        every hair
Is, hair of the head, numbered.
Nay, what we had lighthanded left in surly the mere mould
Will have waked and have waxed and have walked with
        the wind whatwhile we slept,
This side, that side hurling a heavyheaded hundredfold
Whatwhile we, while we slumbered.
O then, weary then whý should we tread ?   O why are we
        so haggard at the heart, so care-coiled, care-killed, so
        fagged, so fashed, so cogged, so cumbered,

When the thing we freely fórfeit is kept with fonder a care,
Fonder a care kept than we could have kept it, kept
Far with fonder a care (and we, we should have lost it)
    finer, fonder
A care kept.—Where kept ?   Do but tell us where kept,
    where.—
Yonder.—What high as that !   We follow, now we follow.
    —Yonder, yes yonder, yonder,
Yonder.

THE CANDLE INDOORS

SOME candle clear burns somewhere I come by.
I muse at how its being puts blissful back
With yellowy moisture mild night's blear-all black,
Or to-fro tender trambeams truckle at the eye.
By that window what task what fingers ply,
I plod wondering, a-wanting, just for lack
Of answer the eagerer a-wanting Jessy or Jack
There.   God to aggrándize, God to glorify.—

Come you indoors, come home ; your fading fire
Mend first and vital candle in close heart's vault :
You there are master, do your own desire ;
What hinders ?   Are you beam-blind, yet to a fault
In a neighbour deft-handed ?   Are you that liar
And cast by conscience out, spendsavour salt ?

THE HORSEMEN *John Alford*

PANTING the horsemen topped the glowing hill.
Before them spread five shafts of an orange sun,
Behind them stood the old rain-rotted mill
Whose sails no longer spun.

The earth smelt new with rain. Their horses steamed
And stirred the silence with a champing bit.
Along the road a few still puddles gleamed
With fires a last ray lit.

One said " To-morrow will be wet again,"
And read the sky with unperturbed gaze.
" Good-night "—they dug their heels and shook a rein
And rode their diverse ways.

EPITAPH *Lascelles Abercrombie*

SIR, you should notice me : I am the Man ;
I am Good Fortune : I am satisfied.
All I desired, more than I could desire,
I have : everything has gone right with me.
Life was a hiding-place that played me false ;
I croucht ashamed, and still was seen and scorned :
But now I am not seen. I was a fool,
And now I know what wisdom dare not know :
For I know Nothing. I was a slave, and now
I have ungoverned freedom and the wealth
That cannot be conceived : for I have Nothing.
I lookt for beauty and I longed for rest,
And now I have perfection : nay, I am
Perfection : I am Nothing, I am dead.

132

THERE lies afar behind a western hill
The Town without a Market, white and still ;
For six feet long and not a third as high
Are those small habitations. There stood I,
Waiting to hear the citizens beneath
Murmur and sigh and speak through tongueless teeth.
When all the world lay burning in the sun
I heard their voices speak to me. Said One :
" Bright lights I loved and colours, I who find
That death is darkness, and has struck me blind."
Another cried : " I used to sing and play,
But here the world is silent, day by day."
And one : " On earth I could not see or hear,
But with my fingers touched what I was near,
And knew things round and soft, and brass from gold,
And dipped my hand in water, to feel cold,
And thought the grave would cure me, and was glad
When the time came to lose what joy I had."
Soon all the voices of a hundred dead
Shouted in wrath together. Some one said,
" I care not, but the girl was sweet to kiss
At evening in the meadows." " Hard it is,"
Another cried, " to hear no hunting horn.
Ah me ! the horse, the hounds, and the great grey morn
When I rode out a-hunting." And one sighed,
" I did not see my son before I died."
A boy said, " I was strong and swift to run :
Now they have tied my feet : what have I done ? "
A man, " But it was good to arm and fight
And storm their cities in the dead of night."
An old man said, " I read my books all day,
But death has taken all my books away."
And one, " The popes and prophets did not well
To cheat poor dead men with false hopes of hell.
Better the whips of fire that hiss and rend

Than painless void proceeding to no end."
I smiled to hear them restless, I who sought
Peace. For I had not loved, I had not fought,
And books are vanities, and manly strength
A gathered flower. God grant us peace at length !
I heard no more, and turned to leave their town
Before the chill came, and the sun went down.
Then rose a whisper, and I seemed to know
A timorous man, buried long years ago.
" On Earth I used to shape the Thing that seems.
Master of all men, give me back my dreams.
Give me that world that never failed me then,
The hills I made and peopled with tall men,
The palace that I built and called my home,
My cities which could break the pride of Rome,
The three queens hidden in the sacred tree,
And those white cloud folk who sang to me.
O death, why hast thou covered me so deep ?
I was thy sister's child, the friend of Sleep."

Then said my heart, Death takes and cannot give.
Dark with no dream is hateful. Let me live !

SEA LOVE
Charlotte Mew

TIDE be runnin' the great world over :
    'T was only last June month I mind that we
Was thinkin' the toss and the call in the breast of the lover
    So everlastin' as the sea.

Heer's the same little fishes that sputter and swim,
    Wi' the moon's old glim on the grey, wet sand ;
An' him no more to me nor me to him
    Than the wind goin' over my hand.

134

I

Happy are men who yet before they are killed
Can let their veins run cold.
Whom no compassion fleers
Or makes their feet
Sore on the alleys cobbled with their brothers
The front line withers,
But they are troops who fade, not flowers
For poets' tearful fooling :
Men, gaps for filling
Losses who might have fought
Longer ; but no one bothers.

II

And some cease feeling
Even themselves or for themselves.
Dullness best solves
The tease and doubt of shelling,
And Chance's strange arithmetic
Comes simpler than the reckoning of their shilling.
They keep no check on Armies' decimation.

III

Happy are these who lose imagination :
They have enough to carry with ammunition.
Their spirit drags no pack.
Their old wounds save with cold can not more ache.
Having seen all things red,
Their eyes are rid
Of the hurt of the colour of blood for ever.
And terror's first constriction over,
Their hearts remain small drawn.
Their senses in some scorching cautery of battle
Now long since ironed,
Can laugh among the dying, unconcerned.

IV

Happy the soldier home, with not a notion
How somewhere, every dawn, some men attack,
And many sighs are drained.
Happy the lad whose mind was never trained :
His days are worth forgetting more than not.
He sings along the march
Which we march taciturn, because of dusk,
The long, forlorn, relentless trend
From larger day to huger night.

V

We wise, who with a thought besmirch
Blood over all our soul,
How should we see our task
But through his blunt and lashless eyes ?
Alive, he is not vital overmuch ;
Dying, not mortal overmuch ;
Nor sad, nor proud,
Nor curious at all.
He cannot tell
Old men's placidity from his.

VI

But cursed are dullards whom no cannon stuns,
That they should be as stones.
Wretched are they, and mean
With paucity that never was simplicity.
By choice they made themselves immune
To pity and whatever mourns in man
Before the last sea and the hapless stars ;
Whatever mourns when many leave these shores ;
Whatever shares
The eternal reciprocity of tears.

HARRY PLOUGHMAN
Gerard Manley Hopkins

HARD as hurdle arms, with a broth of goldish flue
Breathed round ; the rack of ribs ; the scooped flank ;
    lank
Rope-over thigh ; knee-nave ; and barrelled shank—
        Head and foot, shoulder and shank—
By a grey eye's heed steered well, one crew, fall to ;
Stand at stress. Each limb's barrowy brawn, his thew
That onewhere curded, onewhere sucked or sank—
        Soared or sank—,
Though as a beechbole firm, finds his, as at a roll-call rank
And features, in flesh, what deed he each must do—
        His sinew-service where do.

He leans to it, Harry bends, look. Back, elbow, and
    liquid waist
In him, all quail to the wallowing o' the plough : 's cheek
    crimsons ; curls
Wag or crossbridle, in a wind lifted, windlaced—
        See his wind- lilylocks- laced ;
Churlsgrace, too, child of Amansstrength, how it hangs or
    hurls
Them—broad in bluff hide his frowning feet lashed !
    raced
With, along them, cragiron under and cold furls—
        With-a-fountain's shining-shot furls.

JONAH AND THE WHALE
Viola Meynell

HE sported round the watery world.
His rich oil was a gloomy waveless lake
Within the waves. Affrighted seamen hurled
    Their weapons in his foaming wake.

137

One old corroding iron he bore
Which journeyed through his flesh but yet had not
Found out his life. Another lance he wore
Outside him pricking in a tender spot.

So distant were his parts that they
Sent but a dull faint message to his brain.
He knew not his own flesh, as great kings may
Not know the farther places where they reign.

His play made storm in a calm sea ;
His very kindness slew what he might touch ;
And wrecks lay scattered on his anger's lee.
The Moon rocked to and fro his watery couch.

His hunger cleared the sea. And where
He passed, the ocean's edge lifted its brim.
He skimmed the dim sea-floor to find if there
Some garden had its harvest ripe for him.

But in his sluggish brain no thought
Ever arose. His law was instinct blind.
No thought or gleam or vision ever brought
Light to the dark of his old dreamless mind.

Until one day sudden and strange
Half-tints of knowledge burst upon his sight.
Glimpses he had of Time, and Space, and Change,
    And something greater than his might ;

And terror's leap to imagine sin ;
And blinding Truth half-bare unto his seeing.
It was the living man who had come in,—
    Jonah's thoughts flying through his being.

THE PIKE

Edmund Blunden

FROM shadows of rich oaks outpeer
The moss-green bastions of the weir,
Where the quick dipper forages
In elver-peopled crevices,
And a small runlet trickling down the sluice
Gossamer music tires not to unloose.

Else round the broad pools hush
    Nothing stirs,
Unless sometime a straggling heifer crush
Through the thronged spinney where the pheasant whirs ;
  Or martins in a flash
Come with wild mirth to dip their magical wings,
While in the shallow some doomed bulrush swings
At whose hid root the diver vole's teeth gnash.

And nigh this toppling reed, still as the dead
  The great pike lies, the murderous patriarch
  Watching the waterpit sheer-shelving dark,
Where through the plash his lithe bright vassals
    thread.

  The rose-finned roach and bluish bream
  And staring ruffe steal up the stream
  Hard by their glutted tyrant, now
  Still as a sunken bough.

  He on the sandbank lies,
    Sunning himself long hours
  With stony gorgon eyes :
    Westward the hot sun lowers.

Sudden the gray pike changes, and quivering poises for
    slaughter ;
  Intense terror wakens around him, the shoals scud
    awry, but there chances

A chub unsuspecting ; the prowling fins quicken, in
    fury he lances ;
And the miller that opens the hatch stands amazed at
    the whirl in the water.

A LONELY PLACE   *Edward Shanks*

The leafless trees, the untidy stack,
    Last rainy summer raised in haste,
Watch the sky turn from fair to black
    And watch the river fill and waste.

But never a footstep comes to trouble
    The rooks among the new-sown corn
Or pigeons rising from late stubble
    And flashing lighter as they turn.

Or if a footstep comes, 'tis mine,
    Sharp on the road or soft on grass :
Silence divides along my line
    And shuts behind me as I pass.

No other comes, no labourer
    To cut his shaggy truss of hay,
Along the road no traveller,
    Day after day, day after day.

And even I, when I come here,
    Move softly on, subdued and still,
Lonely as death, though I can hear
    Men shouting on the other hill.

Day after day, though no one sees,
    The lonely place no different seems,
The trees, the stack, still images
    Constant in who can say whose dreams ?

'WHO called ? ' I said, and the words
    Through the whispering glades,
Hither, thither, baffled the birds—
    ' Who called ?   Who called ? '

The leafy boughs on high
    Hissed in the sun ;
The dark air carried my cry
    Faintingly on :

Eyes in the green, in the shade,
    In the motionless brake,
Voices that said what I said,
    For mockery's sake :

' Who cares ? ' I bawled through my tears ;
    The wind fell low :
In the silence, ' Who cares ? who cares ? '
    Wailed to and fro.

THE MOTH

ISLED in the midnight air,
Musked with the dark's faint bloom,
Out into glooming and secret haunts
    The flame cries, ' Come ! '

Lovely in dye and fan,
A-tremble in shimmering grace,
A moth from her winter swoon
    Uplifts her face :

Stares from her glamorous eyes ;
Wafts her on plumes like mist ;
In ecstasy swirls and sways
    To her strange tryst.

WHO taught the centaur first to drink
Ladling his huge hands from the brink—
When other monsters lie and lap
The waters like a fruitful pap ?—

The same who by ingenious ways
Taught the chameleon his rays
To take from leaves of tow'ring trees
Strung thick with dew-bells that the bees
Set ringing, till they bring the honey,
Thrilled with music, gold with money
Back to their castles in the clouds—
And the chameleon, his crowds
Of foes to fight with, has two eyes
That travel sideways, no surprise
On any side. He swiftly sees
All—flowers, slow floating birds and bees.

The gentle, loving unicorn
Will never eat the grass—
All bushes have too many thorns,
Their leaves are made of brass.
His horn is given him to take
The soft fruit from the trees.
" Please grasp my horn and roughly shake,
O nymph, among those leaves ;
This pear transfixed upon my horn ;
I cannot reach "—beyond the brim ;
Clutched at ; she misses ; it has gone.
" Alas ! You've got it ! " " I can't swim."

To comb a satyr's silken beard
Arabian travellers aspire,

They beg, they bribe ; more loved than feared
The satyr trots to take his hire—
Fawning, he takes from outstretched hand
Such fruit his eyes have sometimes seen
On swaying branches where the land
Sighs in a soft wind and the green
Leaves shake beneath the nightingale.
Thus cajoled, they can reach his beard
Where gums lie, gathered from the frail
Flowers he feeds on, where no voice is heard.

AT BREAKFAST

" A GLASS of milk as white as your hand,
The foam of seas that lie on the land,
Their grass runs swift in the wind like a wave ;
A cup of this foam :—and then I crave
Snow-bread that the hills have ground their gold to !
    The cheap shepherdess replied,
    Her words still-born—dead drowned by the roar.
A railway engine ran across the field
Galloping like a swift horse down the rails.
As it came quicker the window-panes rattled,
The roof shook side to side : all its beams trembled,
Thundering hoofs were upon us—glass chariots.

THE MOON

THE white nightingale is hidden in the branches
    And heavy leafage of the clouds.
She pours down her song—
Cascades threaded like pearls,
And the winds, her many-noted flutes
Flood forth their harmony.—
But the Earth turns away
Swinging in its air and water-rocked cradle.

'IONE, DEAD THE LONG YEAR'   *Ezra Pound*

EMPTY are the ways,
Empty are the ways of this land
And the flowers
     Bend over with heavy heads.
They bend in vain.
Empty are the ways of this land
     where Ione
Walked once, and now does not walk
But seems like a person just gone.

THE COMING OF WAR: ACTÆON

AN image of Lethe
     and the fields
Full of faint light
  but golden,
Grey cliffs,
    and beneath them
A sea
Harsher than granite,
    unstill, never ceasing ;
High forms
    with the movement of gods,
Perilous aspect ;
  And one said :
' This is Actæon.'
     Actæon of golden greaves !
Over fair meadows,
Over the cool face of that field,
Unstill, ever moving
Hosts of an ancient people,
The silent cortège.

OUT of the earth to rest or range
Perpetual in perpetual change,
The unknown passing through the strange.

Water and saltness held together
To tread the dust and stand the weather
And plough the field and stretch the tether,

To pass the wine-cup and be witty,
Water the sands and build the city,
Slaughter like devils and have pity,

Be red with rage and pale with lust,
Make beauty come, make peace, make trust,
Water and saltness mixed with dust ;

Drive over earth, swim under sea,
Fly in the eagle's secrecy,
Guess where the hidden comets be,

Know all the deathy seeds that still
Queen Helen's beauty, Caesar's will,
And slay them even as they kill ;

Fashion an altar for a rood,
Defile a continent with blood,
And watch a brother starve for food ;

Love like a madman, shaking, blind,
Till self is burnt into a kind
Possession of another mind ;

Brood upon beauty, till the grace
Of beauty with the holy face
Brings peace into the bitter place ;

Probe in the lifeless granites, scan
The stars for hope, for guide, for plan ;
Live as a woman or a man ;

Fasten to lover or to friend,
Until the heart break at the end
The break of death that cannot mend ;

Then to lie useless, helpless, still,
Down in the earth, in dark, to fill
The roots of grass or daffodil.

Down in the earth, in dark, alone,
A mockery of the ghost in bone,
The strangeness, passing the unknown.

Time will go by, that outlasts clocks,
Dawn in the thorps will rouse the cocks,
Sunset be glory on the rocks :

But it, the thing, will never heed
Even the rootling from the seed
Thrusting to suck it for its need.

*　　*　　*

Since moons decay and suns decline,
How else should end this life of mine ?
Water and saltness are not wine.

But in the darkest hour of night
When even the foxes peer for sight,
The byre-cock crows ; he feels the light.

So, in this water mixed with dust,
The byre-cock spirit crows from trust
That death will change because it must ;

For all things change, the darkness changes,
The wandering spirits change their ranges,
The corn is gathered to the granges.

The corn is sown again, it grows ;
The stars burn out, the darkness goes ;
The rhythms change, they do not close.

They change, and we, who pass like foam,
Like dust blown through the streets of Rome,
Change ever, too ; we have no home,

Only a beauty, only a power,
Sad in the fruit, bright in the flower,
Endlessly erring for its hour,

But gathering, as we stray, a sense
Of Life, so lovely and intense,
It lingers when we wander hence,

That those who follow feel behind
Their backs, when all before is blind,
Our joy, a rampart to the mind.

THE SUNFLOWER

Peter Quennell

See, I have bent thee by thy saffron hair,
    O most strange masker,
Towards my face, thy face so full of eyes,
    O almost legendary monster.
Thee of the saffron, circling hair I bend,
Bend by my fingers knotted in thy hair,
    Hair like broad flames.
So—shall I swear by beech husk, spindle-berry,
To break thee, saffron hair and peering eye,
    To have the mastery ?

WHAT deaths men have died, not fighting but impotent.
Hung on the wire, between trenches, burning and freezing,
Groaning for water with armies of men so near ;
The fall over cliff, the clutch at the rootless grass,
The beach rushing up, the whirling, the turning head
    first ;
Stiff writhings of strychnine, taken in error or haste,
Angina pectoris, shudders of the heart ;
Failure and crushing by flying weight to the ground,
Claws and jaws, the stink of a lion's breath ;
Swimming, a white belly, a crescent of teeth,
Agony, and a spirting shredded limb
And crimson blood staining the green water ;
And, horror of horrors, the slow grind on the rack,
The breaking bones, the stretching and bursting skin,
Perpetual fainting and waking to see above
The down-thrust mocking faces of cruel men,
With the power of mercy, who gloat upon shrieks for
    mercy.

O pity me, God ! O God, make tolerable,
Make tolerable the end that awaits for me,
And give me courage to die when the time comes,
When the time comes as it must, however it comes,
That I shrink not nor scream, gripped by the jaws of
    the vice ;
For the thought of it turns me sick, and my heart stands
    still,
Knocks and stands still. O fearful, fearful Shadow,
Kill me, let me die to escape the terror of thee !
A tap. Come in ! Oh, no I am perfectly well,
Only a little tired. Take this one, it's softer.
How are things going with you ? Will you have some
    coffee ?

Well, of course, it's trying sometimes, but never mind,
It will probably be all right.   Carry on, and keep cheerful,
I shouldn't, if I were you, meet trouble half-way,
It is always best to take everything as it comes.

THE INDIAN TO HIS LOVE.   *W. B. Yeats*

THE island dreams under the dawn
And great boughs drop tranquillity ;
The peahens dance on a smooth lawn,
A parrot sways upon a tree,
Raging at his own image in the enamelled sea.

Here we will moor our lonely ship
And wander ever with woven hands,
Murmuring softly lip to lip,
Along the grass, along the sands,
Murmuring how far away are the unquiet lands :

How we alone of mortals are
Hid under quiet bows apart,
While our love grows an Indian star,
A meteor of the burning heart,
One with the tide that gleams, the wings that gleam and
      dart,

The heavy boughs, the burnished dove
That moans and sighs a hundred days :
How when we die our shades may rove,
When eve has hushed the feathered ways,
With vapoury footsole among the water's drowsy blaze.

COMMEMORATION

Henry Newbolt

I SAT by the granite pillar, and sunlight fell
    Where the sunlight fell of old,
And the hour was the hour my heart remembered well,
    And the sermon rolled and rolled
As it used to roll when the place was still unhaunted,
And the strangest tale in the world was still untold.

And I knew that of all this rushing of urgent sound
    That I so clearly heard,
The green young forest of saplings clustered round
    Was heeding not one word :
Their heads were bowed in a still serried patience
Such as an angel's breath could never have stirred.

For some were already away to the hazardous pitch,
    Or lining the parapet wall,
And some were in glorious battle, or great and rich,
    Or throned in a college hall :
And among the rest was one like my own young phantom,
Dreaming for ever beyond my utmost call.

" O Youth," the preacher was crying, " deem not thou
    Thy life is thine alone ;
Thou bearest the will of the ages, seeing how
    They built thee bone by bone,
And within thy blood the Great Age sleeps sepulchred
Till thou and thine shall roll away the stone.

" Therefore the days are coming when thou shalt burn
    With passion whitely hot ;
Rest shall be rest no more ; thy feet shall spurn
    All that thy hand hath got ;
And One that is stronger shall gird thee, and lead thee
    swiftly
Whither, O heart of Youth, thou wouldest not."

And the School passed : and I saw the living and dead
    Set in their seats again,
And I longed to hear them speak of the word that was
    said,
    But I knew that I longed in vain.
And they stretched forth their hands, and the wind of
    the spirit took them
Lightly as drifted leaves on an endless plain.

O PULCHRITUDO

O SAINT whose thousand shrines our feet have trod
    And our eyes loved thy lamp's eternal beam,
Dim earthly radiance of the Unknown God,
    Hope of the darkness, light of them that dream,
Far off, far off and faint, O glimmer on
Till we thy pilgrims from the road are gone,

O Word whose meaning every sense hath sought,
    Voice of the teeming field and grassy mound,
Deep-whispering fountain of the wells of thought,
    Will of the wind and soul of all sweet sound,
Far off, far off and faint, O murmur on
Till we thy pilgrims from the road are gone,

HOMEWARD BOUND

AFTER long labouring in the windy ways,
    On smooth and shining tides
    Swiftly the great ship glides,
    Her storms forgot, her weary watches past ;
Northward she glides, and through the enchanted haze
    Faint on the verge her far hope dawns at last.

The phantom sky-line of a shadowy down,
 Whose pale white cliffs below
 Through sunny mist aglow,
 Like noon-day ghosts of summer moonshine gleam—
Soft as old sorrow, bright as old renown,
 There lies the home of all our mortal dream.

THE TRAVELLING COMPANION

Lord Alfred Douglas

INTO the silence of the empty night
I went, and took my scornèd heart with me,
And all the thousand eyes of heaven were bright;
But Sorrow came and led me back to thee.

I turned my weary eyes towards the sun,
Out of the leaden East like smoke came he.
I laughed and said, " The night is past and done ";
But Sorrow came and led me back to thee.

I turned my face towards the rising moon,
Out of the south she came most sweet to see,
She smiled upon my eyes that loathed the noon ;
But Sorrow came and led me back to thee.

I bent my eyes upon the summer land,
And all the painted fields were ripe for me,
And every flower nodded to my hand ;
But Sorrow came and led me back to thee.

O Love ! O Sorrow ! O desired Despair !
I turned my feet towards the boundless sea,
Into the dark I go and heed not where,
So that I come again at last to thee.

THE MIRACLE OF LIFE
R. A. K. Mason

MIRACULOUS how my life-stream has flowed
  From birth of Birth down through each ancestor,
  Through times of caves, of flint, and bronze and fur ;
When distant dam, delivered of her load,
Scarce guessed, yet without whom I ne'er had trod,
  Saw my old half-brute forbear smile at her,
  And, later, viewed him spring, and lust, and err,
And mate and spawn new sires in new abode,

How little did it need to end it all !
  A little venom here, or there a cleft
In one of many rocks, or a cliff-fall,
  An arrow one shade more to right or left
At any time : some wound, however small—
  And this poor link, of life had been bereft.

THE SPARK'S FAREWELL TO ITS CLAY

WELL, clay, it's strange at last we've come to it—
  After much merriment we must give up
  Our ancient friendship ; no more shall we sup
In pleasant, quiet places, wanly-lit,
Nor wander through the falling rain, sharp-smit
  And buffeted thou, while I within, snug-shut ;
  No longer taste the mingled bitter-sweet cup
Of Life the One Inscrutable has thought fit

To give to us ; no longer know the strife
  That we of old have each to each maintained.
  Now our companionship hath certain end—
End without end. At last of this, our life,
  Thou surely hast gained blank earth walls, my friend—

And I ? God only knows what I have gained.

153

THE fat light clings upon my skin,
Like grease that slowly forms a thin
And foul white film ; so close it lies,
It feeds upon my lips and eyes.

The black fly hits the window-pane
That shuts its dirty body in ;
So once, his spirit fought to quit
The body that imprisoned it.

He always seemed so fond of me,
Until one day he chanced to see
My head, a little on one side,
Loll softly as if I had died.

Since then, he rarely looked my way,
Though he could never know what lay
Within my brain ; though iron his will,
I thought, he's young and teachable.

And often, as I took my drink,
I chuckled in my heart to think
Whose dark blood ran within his veins :
You see, it spared me half my pains.

The time was very long until
I had the chance to work my will ;
Once seen, the way was clear as light,
A father's patience infinite.

He always was so sensitive ;
But soon I taught him how to live
With each day, just a patch of white,
A blinded patch of black, each night.

Each day he watched my gaiety.
It's very difficult to die
When one is young . . . I pitied him,
The glass I filled up to the brim,

His shaking fingers scarce could hold ;
His limbs were trembling as with cold. . . .
I waited till from night and day
All meaning I had wiped away,

And then I gave it him again ;
The wine made heaven in his brain.
Then spider-like, the kindly wine
Thrust tentacles through every vein,

And knotted him so very fast
I knew I had him safe at last.
And sometimes in the dawn, I'd creep
To watch him as he lay asleep,

And each time, see my son's face grown
In some blurred line, more like my own.
A crumpled rag, he lies all night
Until the first white smear of light ;

And sleep is but an empty hole . . .
No place for him to hide his soul,
No outlet there to set him free :
He never can escape from me.

Yet still I never know what thought,
All fly-like in his mind lies caught :
His face seems some half-spoken word
Forgot again as soon as heard,

Beneath the livid skin of light;
Oh, just an empty space of white,
Now all the meaning's gone. I'll sit
A little while and stare at it.

THE COUNTY CALLS

THEY came upon us like a train—
A rush, a scream, then gone again !
With bodies like a continent
Encased in silken seas, they went.

And came and called and took their tea
And patronised the Deity
Who copies their munificence
With creditable heart and sense.

Each face a plaster monument
For some belovèd aliment,
Whose everlasting sleep they deign
To cradle in the Great Inane ;

Each tongue, a noisy clockwork bell
To toll the passing hour that fell ;
Each hat, an architect's device
For building churches, cheap and nice.

I saw the County Families
Advance and sit and take their teas ;
I saw the County gaze askance
At my thin insignificance :

Small thoughts like frightened fishes glide
Beneath their eyes' pale glassy tide :
They said : " Poor thing ! we must be nice ! "
They said : " We know your father ! "—twice.

THE CENTAURS *James Stephens*

PLAYING upon the hill three centaurs were !
They lifted each a hoof ! They stared at me !
And stamped the dust !

They stamped the dust ! They snuffed upon the air !
And all their movements had the fierce glee
Of power, and pride, and lust !

Of power and pride and lust ! Then, with a shout,
They tossed their heads, and wheeled, and galloped
    round,
In furious brotherhood !

In furious brotherhood ! Around, about,
They charged, they swerved, they leaped !
    Then, bound on bound,
They raced into the wood !

THE DEED (II) *T. Sturge Moore*

No sight earth yields our eyes is lovelier than
The body of a naked strong young man.
O watch him course the meadows flecked with shade
Beside a stream, before his plunge be made !
Then watch him ridge the water to its brims
With rhythmic measure while he gravely swims ;
And watch him issue, shining even more,
Run, leap and prove himself upon the shore,
Intent to warm his limbs and have them dry,
Making great efforts, seeming as he would fly.
Ah ! he can fill an hour up in this way
And never hear a voice within him say
" Why art thou not at work ? " for it is true
That all he is approves what he doth do.

157

It's my fear that my wake won't be quiet,
　Nor my wake-house a silent place:
For who would keep back the hundreds
　Who would touch my breast and my face?

For the good men were always my friends,
　From Galway back into Clare.
In strength, in sport, and in spending,
　I was foremost at the fair.

In music, in song, and in friendship,
　In contests by night and by day,
By all who knew it was given to me
　That I bore the branch away.

Now let Manus Joyce, my friend
　(If he be at all in the place),
Make smooth the boards of the coffin
　They will put above my face.

The old men will have their stories
　Of all the deeds in my days,
And the young men will stand by the coffin
　And be sure and clear in my praise.

But the girls will stay near the door,
　And they'll have but little to say:
They'll bend their heads, the young girls,
　And for a while they will pray.

And, going home in the dawning,
　They'll be quiet with the boys:
The girls will walk together,
　And seldom they'll lift the voice.

And then, between daybreak and dark,
　And between the hill and the sea,

Three Women, come down from the Mountain,
 Will raise the Keen over me.

But 'tis my grief that I will not hear
 When the cuckoo cries in Glenart,
That the wind that lifts when the sails are loosed
 Will never lift my heart.

THE LION

W. J. Turner

STRANGE spirit with inky hair,
 Tail tufted stiff in rage,
I saw with sudden stare
 Leap on the printed page.

The stillness of its roar
 From midnight deserts torn
Clove silence to the core
 Like the blare of a great horn.

I saw the sudden sky ;
 Cities in crumbling sand ;
The stars fall wheeling by ;
 The lion roaring stand :

The stars fall wheeling by,
 Their silent, silver stain,
Cold on his glittering eye,
 Cold on his carven mane.

The full-orbed Moon shone down,
 The silence was so loud,
From jaws wide-open thrown
 His voice hung like a cloud.

Earth shrank to blackest air ;
 That spirit stiff in rage
Into some midnight lair
 Leapt from the printed page.

THE RAINY SUMMER

Alice Meynell

There's much afoot in heaven and earth this year ;
  The winds hunt up the sun, hunt up the moon,
Trouble the dubious dawn, hasten the drear
  Height of a threatening noon.

No breath of boughs, no breath of leaves, of fronds
  May linger or grow warm ; the trees are loud ;
The forest, rooted, tosses in her bonds,
  And strains against the cloud.

No scents may pause within the garden-fold ;
  The rifled flowers are cold as ocean-shells ;
Bees, humming in the storm, carry their cold
  Wild honey to cold cells.

THE LINNET

Walter de la Mare

Upon this leafy bush
  With thorns and roses in it,
Flutters a thing of light,
  A twittering linnet,
And all the throbbing world
  Of dew and sun and air
By this small parcel of life
  Is made more fair ;
As if each bramble-spray
  And mounded gold-wreathed furze,
Harebell and little thyme,
  Were only hers ;
As if this beauty and grace
  Did to one bird belong,
And, at a flutter of wing,
  Might vanish in song.

THE STARLING Ford Madox Hueffer

IT's an odd thing how one changes . . .
Walking along the upper ranges
Of this land of plains,
In this month of rains,
On a drying road where the poplars march along,
Suddenly,
With a rush of wings flew down a company,
A multitude, throng upon throng,
Of starlings,
Successive orchestras of song,
Flung, like the babble of surf,
On to the roadside turf—

And so, for a mile, for a mile and a half—a long way,
Flight follows flight
Thro' the still grey light
Of the steel-grey day,
Whirling beside the road in clamorous crowds,
Never near, never far, in the shade of the poplars and
    clouds.

It's an odd thing how one changes . . .
And what strikes me now as most strange is :
After the starlings had flown
Over the plain and were gone,
There was one of them stayed on alone
In the trees ; it chattered on high,
Lifting its bill to the sky,
Distending its throat,
Crooning harsh note after note,
In soliloquy,
Sitting alone.
And after a hush

It gurgled as gurgles a well,
Warbled as warbles a thrush,
Had a try at the sound of a bell
And mimicked a jay. . . .
But I,
Whilst the starling mimicked on high
Pulsing its throat and its wings,
I went on my way
Thinking of things,
Onwards and over the range
And that's what is strange.

I went down 'twixt tobacco and grain,
Descending the chequer board plain
Where the apples and maize are ;
Under the loopholed gate
In the village wall
Where the goats clatter over the cobbles
And the intricate, straw-littered ways are . . .
The ancient watchman hobbles
Cloaked, with his glasses of horn at the end of his nose,
Wearing velvet short hose
And a three-cornered hat on his pate,
And his pike-staff and all.
And he carries a proclamation,
An invitation,
To great and small,
Man and beast
To a wedding feast,
And he carries a bell and rings . . .
From the steeple looks down a saint,
From a doorway a queenly peasant
Looks out, in her bride-gown of lace
And her sister, a quaint little darling
Who twitters and chirps like a starling.

And this little old place,
It's so quaint,
It's so pleasant ;
And the watch bell rings, and the church bell rings
And the wedding procession draws nigh,
Bullock cars, fiddlers and goods.
But I
Pass on my way to the woods
Thinking of things.

Years ago I'd have stayed by the starling,
Marking the irridescence of his throat,
Marvelling at the change of his note ;
I'd have said to the peasant child : " Darling
Here's a groschen and give me a kiss " . . . I'd have
    stayed
To sit with the bridesmaids at table,
And have taken my chance
Of a dance,
With the bride in her laces
Or the maids with the blonde, placid faces
And ribbons and crants in the stable . . .

But the church bell still rings
And I'm far away out on the plain,
In the grey weather amongst the tobacco and grain,
And village and gate and wall
Are a long grey line with the church over all
And miles and miles away in the sky
The starlings go wheeling round on high
Over the distant ranges.
The violin strings
Thrill away and the day grows more grey.
And I . . . I stand thinking of things.
Yes, it's strange how one changes.

THE HILLS
Frances Cornford

OUT of the complicated house, come I
To walk beneath the sky.
Here mud and stones and turf, here everything
Is mutely comforting.
Now hung upon the twigs and thorns appear
A host of lovely rain-drops cold and clear.
And on the bank
Or deep in brambly hedges dank
The small birds nip about, and say :
" Brothers, the Spring is not so far away ! "
The hills like mother-giantesses old
Lie in the cold.
And with a complete patience, let
The cows come cropping on their bosoms wet,
And even tolerate that such as I
Should wander by
With paltry leathern heel which cannot harm
Their bodies calm ;
And, with a heart they cannot know, to bless
The enormous power of their peacefulness.

THE CUCKOO
Vivian Locke Ellis

COME early, Cuckoo, patient bird,
And on thy three-stringed viol strum ;
Come early, Cuckoo : thou art heard,
And no man doubts that spring hath come ;
Tune thy two strings and break the third.

Come seldom, Cuckoo, welcome guest
Who wear'st thy welcome out too soon ;
Usurper of the small bird's nest,
Thou art well paid for thy one tune.
Now get thee gone, thou weariest.

SEAGULLS ON THE SERPENTINE   *Alfred Noyes*

MEMORY, out of the mist, in a long slow ripple
  Breaks, blindly, against the shore.
The mist has buried the town in its own oblivion.
  This, this is the sea once more.

Mist—mist—brown mist; but a sense in the air of
    snow-flakes !
  I stand where the ripples die,
Lift up an arm and wait, till my lost ones know me,
  Wheel overhead, and cry.

Salt in the eyes, and the seagulls, mewing and swooping,
  Snatching the bread from my hand ;
Brushing my hand with their breasts, in swift caresses
  To show that they understand.

Oh, why are you so afraid ? We are all of us exiles !
  Wheel back in your clamorous rings !
We have all of us lost the sea, and we all remember.
  But you—have wings.

WHAT THE SHUILER SAID AS SHE LAY BY THE FIRE IN THE FARMER'S HOUSE   *Padraic Colum*

I'M glad to lie on a sack of leaves
By a wasted fire and take my ease.
For the wind would strip me bare as a tree—
The wind would blow old age upon me.
And I'm dazed with the wind, the rain, and the cold.
  If I had only the good red gold
To buy me the comfort of a roof,
And under the thatch the brown of the smoke !
  I'd lie up in my painted room
Until my hired girl would come ;

And when the sun had warmed my walls
I'd rise up in my silks and shawls,
And break my fast before the fire.
And I'd watch them that had to sweat
And shiver for shelter and what they ate.
The farmer digging in the fields ;
The beggars going from gate to gate ;
The horses striving with their loads,
And all the sights upon the roads.

I'd live my lone without clan or care,
And none about me to crave a share.
The young have mocking, impudent ways,
And I'd never let them a-nigh my place.
And a child has often a pitiful face.
  I'd give the rambling fiddler rest,
And for me he would play his best.
And he'd have something to tell of me
From the Moat of Granard down to the sea !
And, though I'd keep distant, I'd let in
Old women who would card and spin
And clash with me, and I'd hear it said,
  "Mór who used to carry her head
As if she was a lady bred—
Has little enough in her house, they say—
And such-a-one's child I saw on the way
Scaring crows from a crop, and glad to get,
In a warmer house, the bit to eat.
O ! none are safe, and none secure,
And it's well for some whose bit is sure ! "

  I'd never grudge them the weight of their lands
If I had only the good red gold
To huggle between my breast and hands !

BASE DETAILS

If I were fierce and bald and short of breath,
  I'd live with scarlet Majors at the Base,
And speed glum heroes up the line to death.
  You'd see me with my puffy petulant face,
Guzzling and gulping in the best hotel,
  Reading the Roll of Honour. "Poor young chap,"
I'd say—"I used to know his father well;
  Yes, we've lost heavily in this last scrap."
And when the war is done and youth stone dead,
I'd toddle safely home and die—in bed.

THE DUG-OUT

Why do you lie with your legs ungainly huddled,
And one arm bent across your sullen cold
Exhausted face? It hurts my heart to watch you,
Deep-shadow'd from the candle's guttering gold:
And you wonder why I shake you by the shoulder;
Drowsy, you mumble and sigh and shift your head. . . .
You are too young to fall asleep for ever;
And when you sleep you remind me of the dead.

SUICIDE IN TRENCHES

I knew a simple soldier boy
Who grinned at life in empty joy,
Slept soundly through the lonesome dark,
And whistled early with the lark.

In winter trenches, cowed and glum
With crumps and lice and lack of rum,

167

He put a bullet through his brain.
No one spoke of him again.

*   *   *

You smug-faced crowds with kindling eye
Who cheer when soldier lads march by,
Sneak home and pray you'll never know
The hell where youth and laughter go.

THE GLORY OF WOMEN

You love us when we're heroes, home on leave,
Or wounded in a mentionable place.
You worship decorations ; you believe
That chivalry redeems the war's disgrace.
You make us shells. You listen with delight,
By tales of dirt and danger fondly thrilled.
You crown our distant ardours while we fight,
And mourn our laurelled memories when we're killed.

You can't believe that British troops ' retire '
When hell's last horror breaks them, and they run,
Trampling the terrible corpses—blind with blood.
O German mother dreaming by the fire,
While you are knitting socks to send your son
His face is trodden deeper in the mud.

MEMORIAL TABLET (GREAT WAR)

SQUIRE nagged and bullied till I went to fight
(Under Lord Derby's scheme). I died in hell—
(They call it Passchendaele) ; my wound was slight,
And I was hobbling back, and then a shell
Burst slick upon the duck-boards ; so I fell
Into the bottomless mud, and lost the light.

In sermon-time, while Squire is in his pew,
He gives my gilded name a thoughtful stare ;
For though low down upon the list, I'm there :
" In proud and glorious memory "—that's my due.
Two bleeding years I fought in France for Squire ;
I suffered anguish that he's never guessed ;
Once I came home on leave ; and then went west.
What greater glory could a man desire ?

THE SISTERS

Roy Campbell

AFTER hot loveless nights, when cool winds stream
Sprinkling the frost and dew, before the light,
Bored with the foolish things that girls must dream
Because their beds are empty of delight,

Two sisters rise and strip. Out from the night
Their horses run to their low-whistled pleas—
Vast phantom shapes, with eyeballs rolling white,
That sneeze a fiery steam about their knees.

Through the crisp manes their stealthy prowling hands,
Stronger than curbs, in slow caresses rove—
They gallop down across the milkwhite sands
And wade far out into the sleeping cove.

The frost stings sweetly with a burning kiss,
As intimate as love, as cold as death :
Their lips, whereon delicious tremors hiss,
Fume with the ghostly pollen of their breath.

Far out in the grey silence of the flood
They watch the dawn in smouldering gyres expand
Beyond them : and the day burns through their blood
Like a white candle through a shuttered hand.

LATE SNOW

J. C. Squire

THE heavy train through the dim country went rolling,
   rolling,
Interminably passing misty snow-covered ploughland
   ridges
That merged in the snowy sky ; came turning meadows,
   fences,
Came gullies and passed, and ice-coloured streams under
   frozen bridges.

Across the travelling landscape evenly drooped and
   lifted
The telegraph wires, thick ropes of snow in the windless
   air ;
They drooped and paused and lifted again to unseen
   summits,
Drawing the eyes and soothing them, often to a drowsy
   stare.

Singly in the snow the ghosts of trees were softly
   pencilled,
Fainter and fainter, in distance fading, into nothingness
   gliding,
But sometimes a crowd of the intricate silver trees of
   fairyland
Passed, close and intensely clear, the phantom world
   hiding.

O untroubled these moving mantled miles of shadowless
   shadows,
And lovely the film of falling flakes, so wayward and
   slack ;
But I thought of many a mother-bird screening her
   nestlings,
Sitting silent with wide bright eyes, snow on her back.

WHILE joy gave clouds the light of stars,
  That beamed where'er they looked;
And calves and lambs had tottering knees,
  Excited, while they sucked;
While every bird enjoyed his song,
Without one thought of harm or wrong—
I turned my head and saw the wind,
  Not far from where I stood,
Dragging the corn by her golden hair,
  Into a dark and lonely wood.

TO SPARROWS FIGHTING

STOP, feathered bullies!
  Peace, angry birds;
You common Sparrows that,
  For a few words,
Roll fighting in wet mud,
To shed each other's blood.

Look at those Linnets, they
  Like ladies sing;
See how those Swallows, too,
  Play on the wing;
All other birds close by
Are gentle, clean and shy.

And yet maybe your life's
  As sweet as theirs;
The common poor that fight
  Live not for years
In one long frozen state
Of anger, like the great.

171

THE ROLLING ENGLISH ROAD *G. K. Chesterton*

BEFORE the Roman came to Rye or out to Severn strode,
The rolling English drunkard made the rolling English
road.
A reeling road, a rolling road, that rambles round the
shire,
And after him the parson ran, the sexton and the squire ;
A merry road, a mazy road, and such as we did tread
The night we went to Birmingham by way of Beachy
Head.

I knew no harm of Bonaparte and plenty of the Squire,
And for to fight the Frenchman I did not much desire ;
But I did bash their baggonets because they came
arrayed
To straighten out the crooked road an English drunkard
made,
Where you and I went down the lane with ale-mugs
in our hands,
The night we went to Glastonbury by way of Goodwin
Sands.

His sins they were forgiven him ; or why do flowers run
Behind him ; and the hedges all strengthening in the
sun ?
The wild thing went from left to right and knew not
which was which,
But the wild rose was above him when they found him
in the ditch.
God pardon us, nor harden us ; we did not see so clear
The night we went to Bannockburn by way of Brighton
Pier.

My friends, we will not go again or ape an ancient rage,
Or stretch the folly of our youth to be the shame of age,
But walk with clearer eyes and ears this path that
    wandereth,
And see undrugged in evening light the decent inn of
    death ;
For there is good news yet to hear and fine things to be
    seen,
Before we go to Paradise by way of Kensal Green.

DRUGGED   *Walter de la Mare*

INERT in his chair,
In a candle's guttering glow ;
His bottle empty,
His fire sunk low ;
With drug-sealed lids shut fast,
Unsated mouth ajar,
This darkened phantasm walks
Where nightmares are :

In a frenzy of life and light,
Crisscross—a menacing throng—
They gibe, they squeal at the stranger,
Jostling along,
Their faces cadaverous grey.
While on high from an attic stare
Horrors, in beauty apparelled,
Down the dark air

A stream gurgles over its stones,
The chambers within are a-fire.
Stumble his shadowy feet
Through shine, through mire ;
And the flames leap higher.

In vain yelps the wainscot mouse ;
In vain beats the hour ;
Vacant, his body must drowse
Until daybreak flower—

Staining these walls with its rose,
And the draughts of the morning shall stir
Cold on cold brow, cold hands.
And the wanderer
Back to flesh house must return.
Lone soul—in horror to see,
Than dream more meagre and awful,
Reality.

PRELUDES (I)   *T. S. Eliot*

THE winter evening settles down
With smells of steaks in passageways.
Six o'clock.
The burnt-out ends of smoky days.
And now a gusty shower wraps
The grimy scraps
Of withered leaves about your feet
And newspapers from vacant lots ;
The showers beat
On broken blinds and chimney-pots,
And at the corner of the street
A lonely cab-horse steams and stamps.
And then the lighting of the lamps.

THE HAWK

THE hawk slipt out of the pine, and rose in the sunlit air :
Steady and still he poised ; his shadow slept on the grass :
And the bird's song sickened and sank : she cowered
  with furtive stare
Dumb, till the quivering dimness should flicker and shift
  and pass.

Suddenly down he dropped : she heard the hiss of his
  wing,
Fled with a scream of terror : oh, would she had dared
  to rest !
For the hawk at eve was full, and there was no bird to
  sing,
And over the heather drifted the down from a bleeding
  breast.

THE PHŒNIX

By feathers green, across Casbeen,
  The pilgrims track the Phœnix flown,
By gems he strewed in waste and wood,
  And jewelled plumes at random thrown.

Till wandering far, by moon and star,
  They stand beside the fruitful pyre,
Whence breaking bright with sanguine light,
  The impulsive bird forgets his sire.

Those ashes shine like ruby wine,
  Like bag of Tyrian murex spilt,
The claw, the jowl of the flying fowl
  Are with the glorious anguish gilt.

So rare the light, so rich the sight,
  Those pilgrim men, on profit bent,
Drop hands and eyes and merchandise,
  And are with gazing most content.

175

'Twas fifty quatrains : and from unknown strands
The woman came who sang them on the floor.
I saw her, I was leaning by the door,
—Saw her strange raiment and her lovely hands ;
And saw . . . but *that* I think she sang—the bands
Of low-voiced women on a happy shore :
Incomparable was the haze, and bore
The many blossoms of soft orchard lands.
'Twas fifty quatrains, for I caught the measure ;
And all the royal house was full of kings,
Who listened and beheld her and were dumb ;
Nor dared to seize the marvellous rich pleasure,
Too fearful even to ask in whisperings,
The ramparts being closed, whence she had come.

A KISS

David's Reconciliation with Absalom

The fury of a creature when it drips
Wet-fanged, and thirsty with the desert dust,
The clench in battle on a sword that must
Ravish the foe, the pang of finger tips—
Joy of a captain in recovered ships,
Joy, verity of a long-buried lust
Delightsome to the flesh, is in the thrust
Toward Absalom of the king's tarried lips.
And, lo, beneath that awful benison,
A thief's face glittered, sniffing at the gems
Of the bent crown as they were cassia-stems ;
While the young years heard but the rolling on
Of chariots, and a tumult, broke amain
By rumour of an agèd monarch slain.

AT AN INN *John Drinkwater*

WE are talkative, proud, and assured, and self-sufficient,
 The quick of the earth this day ;
This inn is ours, and its courtyard, and English history,
 And the Post Office up the way.

The stars in their changes, and heavenly speculation,
 The habits of birds and flowers,
And character bred of poverty and riches,
 All these are ours.

The world is ours, and these its themes and its substance,
 And of these we are free men and wise ;
Among them all we move in possession and judgment,
 For a day, till it dies.

But in eighteen-hundred-and-fifty, who were the tenants,
 Sure and deliberate as we ?
They knew us not in the time of their ascension,
 Their self-sufficiency.

And in nineteen-hundred-and-fifty this inn shall flourish,
 And history still be told,
And the heat of blood shall thrive, and speculation,
 When we are cold.

COCK-CROW *Edward Thomas*

OUT of the wood of thoughts that grow by night
To be cut down by the sharp axe of light,—
Out of the night, two cocks together crow,
Cleaving the darkness with a silver blow.
And bright before my eyes twin trumpeters stand,
Heralds of splendour, one at either hand,
Each facing each as in a coat-of-arms :
The milkers lace their boots up at the farms.

Robert Graves

OWLS : they whinney down the night,
    Bats go zigzag by.
Ambushed in shadow out of sight
    The outlaws lie.

Old gods, shrunk to shadows, there
    In the wet woods they lurk,
Greedy of human stuff to snare
    In webs of murk.

Look up, else your eye must drown
    In a moving sea of black
Between the tree-tops, upside down
    Goes the sky-track.

Look up, else your feet will stray
    Towards that dim ambuscade,
Where spider-like they catch their prey
    In nets of shade.

For though creeds whirl away in dust,
    Faith fails and men forget,
These aged gods of fright and lust
    Cling to life yet.

Old gods almost dead, malign,
    Starved of their ancient dues,
Incense and fruit, fire, blood and wine
    And an unclean muse.

Banished to woods and a sickly moon,
    Shrunk to mere bogey things,
Who spoke with thunder once at noon
    To prostrate kings.

With thunder from an open sky
  To peasant, tyrant, priest,
Bowing in fear with a dazzled eye
  Towards the East.

Proud gods, humbled, sunk so low,
  Living with ghosts and ghouls,
And ghosts of ghosts and last year's snow
  And dead toadstools.

LOST LOVE

His eyes are quickened so with grief,
He can watch a grass or leaf
Every instant grow ; he can
Clearly through a flint wall see,
Or watch the startled spirit flee
From the throat of a dead man.
  Across two counties he can hear,
And catch your words before you speak.
The woodlouse or the maggot's weak
Clamour rings in his sad ear ;
And noise so slight it would surpass
Credence :—drinking sound of grass,
Worm talk, clashing jaws of moth
Chumbling holes in cloth :
The groan of ants who undertake
Gigantic loads for honour's sake,
Their sinews creak, their breath comes thin :
Whir of spiders when they spin,
And minute whispering, mumbling, sighs
Of idle grubs and flies.
  This man is quickened so with grief,
He wanders god-like or like thief
Inside and out, below, above,
Without relief seeking lost love.

A MEMORY OF THE PLAYERS IN
A MIRROR AT MIDNIGHT

James Joyce

THEY mouth love's language. Gnash
The thirteen teeth
Your lean jaws grin with. Lash
Your itch and quailing, nude greed of the flesh.
Love's breath in you is stale, worded or sung,
As sour as cat's breath,
Harsh of tongue.

This grey that stares
Lies not, stark skin and bone.
Leave greasy lips their kissing. None
Will choose her what you see to mouth upon.
Dire hunger holds his hour.
Pluck forth your heart, saltblood, a fruit of tears,
Pluck and devour !

ON THE BEACH AT FONTANA

WIND whines and whines the shingle,
The crazy pierstakes groan ;
A senile sea numbers each single
Slimesilvered stone.

From whining wind and colder
Grey sea I wrap him warm
And touch his trembling fineboned shoulder
And boyish arm.

Around us fear, descending
Darkness of fear above
And in my heart how deep unending
Ache of love !

180

FROM the doorway when she crept,
Head abased and hand that kept
The shining shaking cloak around her,
The golden cloak that light enwound her
    Neck to knees,

Lone she moved ; no other stirred,
No forbidden foot she heard,
No voice whispered as she passed
'Neath the morning shadow, cast
    Like a darker cloak.

No eye in a wanton glimpse
Sought the whiteness of her limbs,
No look scorched her with its fire
Covetous with wild desire
    As she rode.

All that silence was her praise,
Eyes adored her when their gaze
Sank beneath the throbbing lid.
Glowed her beauty as she hid
    Beauty in her hair.

Golden-cloaked she rode, and now
Raised the brightness of her brow,
Drooped no more the tenderest eyes
Ever moist for miseries ;
    Proud she looked.

Champed her horse the gilded bit,
Tossed his gilded head with wit
Of her gentleness, and paced
Proud with her that now outfaced
    The sun's bright stare.

But one moment—one—she faltered,
Fell her look, her face was altered.
Was it the wind in her hair ?
What unseen hand made a bare
    Roundness of her breast ?

Like a tree that hangs so still,
When no breath falls from the hill,
So she hung ; then moved again,
Along the silent eyeless lane
    Riding on

As though the horse moved with her thought,
And paused when some quick wonder caught
At her heart ; then, as she sighed,
Breathed anew with nostrils wide
    And stepping slow was gone.

Knew she it was I that stirred
The golden cloak, my breath that bared
Half the roundness of her breast ?
Mine the unseen lips that pressed
    Soft as rain ;

My eye that burned with sudden heat
And stung her thought with other sweet ?
Not the wind, but love's swift wild
Fire invisible, undefiled,
    Pleading in love's tongue ?

      .   .   .   .   .

In the hush a bell clapped loud,
Crawled a wan and anxious crowd
Up and down and wantoning
Again with hope, while children cling
    And whimper yet.

But in the Castle's sullen walls
Godiva in a dark dream falls,
Then shady-gowned sits with her Lord,
Sick with thought and newly gored
      By his lust abhorred.

DEIRDRE   *James Stephens*

Do not let any woman read this verse !
It is for men, and after them their sons,
And their sons' sons !

The time comes when our hearts sink utterly ;
When we remember Deirdre and her tale,
And that her lips are dust.

Once she did tread the earth : men took her hand ;
They looked into her eyes and said their say,
And she replied to them.

More than two thousand years it is since she
Was beautiful : she trod the waving grass ;
She saw the clouds.

Two thousand years ! The grass is still the same ;
The clouds as lovely as they were that time
When Deirdre was alive.

But there has been again no woman born
Who was so beautiful ; not one so beautiful
Of all the women born.

Let all men go apart and mourn together !
No man can ever love her ! Not a man
Can dream to be her lover !

No man can bend before her! No man say—
What could one say to her? There are no words
That one could say to her!

Now she is but a story that is told
Beside the fire! No man can ever be
The friend of that poor queen!

THE HOUSE OF GHOSTS   *Humbert Wolfe*

FIRST to describe the house. Who has not seen it
    once at the end of an evening's walk—the leaves
that suddenly open, and as sudden screen it
    with the first flickering hint of shadowy eaves?

Was there a light in the high window? Or
    only the moon's cool candle palely lit?
Was there a pathway leading to the door?
    Or only grass and none to walk on it?

And surely someone cried, " Who goes there—who? "
    And ere the lips could shape the whispered " I,"
the same voice rose, and chuckled, " You, 'tis you! "
    A voice, or the furred night-owl's human cry?

Who has not seen the house? Who has not started
    towards the gate half-seen, and paused, half-fearing,
and half beyond all fear—and the leaves parted
    again, and there was nothing in the clearing?

THE BUILDERS

Laurence Binyon

STAGGERING slowly, and swaying
Heavily at each slow foot's lift and drag,
With tense eyes careless of the roar and throng,
That under jut and jag
Of half-built wall and scaffold streams along,
Six bowed men straining strong
Bear, hardly lifted, a huge lintel stone.
This ignorant thing and prone,
Mere dumbness, blindly weighing,
A brute piece of blank death, a bone
Of the stark mountain, helpless and inert,
Yet draws each sinew till the hot veins swell
And sweat-drops upon hand and forehead start,
Till with short pants the suffering heart
Throbs to the throat, where fiercely hurt
Crushed shoulders cannot heave ; till thought and sense
Are nerved and narrowed to one aim intense,
One effort scarce to be supported longer !
What tyrant will in man or God were stronger
To summon, thrall and seize
The exaction of life's uttermost resource
That from the down-weighed breast and aching knees
To arms lifted in pain
And hands that grapple and strain,
Upsurges, thrusting desperate to repel
The pressure and the force
Of this, which neither feels, nor hears, nor sees ?

THE SHIP OF FAME

Vivian Locke Ellis

FAME waits for me
Out in the offing of the unknown sea.
Her sails are furled,
And at her cable's end she holds the world.

Staunch is the ship
That in the cradle of the sky shall dip
Fire out of foam
And light from stars ; but earth is nearer home.

Dear is the place
Where the white storm drops in the goalless race ;
The harbour-bar
Where the small traders and the fishers are.

And still she rides
High-masted and aloof from sandy tides.
And still they wait,
The chartered boatmen at the harbour gate.

They wait for aye ;
And the shipmaster bides another day.
And sea-things feel
Their way along the roof of crusting keel.

And now and then
The sails of great and lonely merchantmen
'Twixt sea and sky
Hang for awhile, and pass uncertain by.

Sometime, at last,
When the black winter wind is gathering fast,
And no foot falls
On the night shore, nor voice of parting calls,

I shall make haste,
And on the shipboat's benches, sea-ward faced,
Sit rapt and still,
And let the shipmen take me where they will.

HERO ENTOMBED (I)   *Peter Quennell*

My lamp, full charged with its sweet oil, still burns,
Has burned a whole year and it shows no check.
My cerements there
Lie where I rolled them off,
The death odours within them,
Harshly composed, coiled up in marble fold.

This tent of white translucent stone, my tomb,
Lets through its panel such a ray of light,
Blind and refracted,
As a calm sea might do
Through its tough warping lens
From the ascendant moon at its highest step.

Some have complained the gentleness of the sea,
Stagnantly streaming, in quick ebb withdrawing
Along the tideless South,
Thus sound to me,
And like its noonday hiss
Wheels, voices, music, thunder, the trumpet at dawn.

You must not think my entertainment slight
In the close prison where I walk all day.
' And yet, entombed,
Do not your thoughts oppressed
Pluck off the bandage from your sores,
From arrow wound and from ulcered armour-gall ? '

My wounds are dried already to pale weals,
I did not fall in battle as you think,
On Epipolæ
Dashed from the rock head down,
Or in the quarries stifle,
But stoned by words and pierced with beams of eyes.

So, patient, not regretful, self-consoling
I walk, touching the tomb wall with my fingers,
In silent entertainment.
On the smooth floor
The stirred dust ankle deep
Steams up languid, to clog the struggling lamp flame.

MORNING EXPRESS
Siegfried Sassoon

ALONG the wind-swept platform, pinched and white,
The travellers stand in pools of wintry light,
Offering themselves to morn's long, slanting arrows.
The train's due ; porters trundle laden barrows.
The train steams in, volleying resplendent clouds
Of sun-blown vapour. Hither and about,
Scared people hurry, storming the doors in crowds.
The officials seem to waken with a shout,
Resolved to hoist and plunder ; some to the vans
Leap ; others rumble the milk in gleaming cans.

Boys, indolent-eyed, from baskets leaning back,
Question each face ; a man with a hammer steals
Stooping from coach to coach ; with clang and clack,
Touches and tests, and listens to the wheels.
Guard sounds a warning whistle, points to the clock
With brandished flag, and on his folded flock
Claps the last door : the monster grunts : " Enough ! "
Tightening his load of links with pant and puff.
Under the arch, then forth into blue day,
Glide the processional windows on their way,
And glimpse the stately folk who sit at ease
To view the world like kings taking the seas
In prosperous weather : drifting banners tell
Their progress to the counties ; with them goes
The clamour of their journeying ; while those
Who sped them stand to wave a last farewell.

MR. AND MRS. SOUTHERN (Extract) *Osbert Sitwell*

(1) MRS. SOUTHERN'S ENEMY

*   *   *   *

I SEEM to see again
That grey typhoon we knew as Mrs. Southern,
Spinning along the darkened passages,
Watching things, tugging things,
Seeing to things,
                And putting things to rights.

*   *   *   *

Her hair lay coiled and tame at the back of her head.
But her actual majesty was really the golden glory,
Through which she moved, a hurrying fly
Enshrined in rolling amber,
As she spun along in a twisting column of golden atoms,
A halo of gold motes above and about her,
A column of visible, virtuous activity.
Her life was a span of hopeless conflict,
For she battled against Time,
That never-vanquished and invisible foe,
She did not recognize her enemy,
She thought him Dust :
But what is Dust,
Save Time's most lethal weapon,
His faithful ally and our sneaking foe,
Through whom Time steals and covers all we know,
The very instrument through whom he overcame
Great Nineveh and Rome and Carthage,
Ophir and Trebizond and Ephesus,
Now deep, all deep, so deep in dust ?
        Even the lean and arid archæologist,
        Who bends above the stones, and peers and ponders,
        Will be his, too, one day.
Dust loads the dice,
Then challenges to play,

189

Each layer of dust upon a chair or table
A tablet to his future victory.
And Dust is cruel, no victory despising,
However slight,
And Dust is greedy, eats the very bones ;
So that, in the end, still not content
With trophies such as Helen of Troy,
Or with the conquering golden flesh of Cleopatra,
  (She, perhaps, understood the age-long battle,
   For did she not prefer to watch her pearl
   Dissolve in amber wine,
   Thus herself enjoying
   Its ultimate disintegration,
   Than let Dust conquer such a thing of beauty ?
   Was not the asp, fruit-hidden,
   The symbol of such understanding ?),
He needs must seize on Mrs. Southern,
Poor mumbling, struggling, blue-lipped Mrs. Southern,
For Dust is insatiate and invincible.

THE BLACKBIRD

Camilla Doyle

  His notes come through the apple-tree
  Flowing with a leisurely
  Cool and suave limpidity ;

  Deliberately they glide and swing,
  As if he had not only Spring
  But centuries in which to sing.

  He'll pause between each tune as though
  Knowing so many made him slow
  To choose which next shall shine and flow.

  And the golden globes, the dancing spots
  Of light through leaves' opaquer blots,
  Seem the bodies of those golden notes.

WHEN you and I go down
Breathless and cold,
Our faces both worn back
To earthly mould,
How lonely we shall be !
What shall we do,
You without me,
I without you ?

I cannot bear the thought,
You, first, may die,
Nor of how you will weep,
Should I.
We are too much alone ;
What can we do
To make our bodies one :
You, me ; I, you ?

We are most nearly born
Of one same kind ;
We have the same delight,
The same true mind.
Must we then part, we part
Is there no way
To keep a beating heart,
And light of day ?

I could now rise and run
Through street on street
To where you are breathing—you,
That we might meet,
And that your living voice
Might sound above
Fear, and we two rejoice
Within our love.

How frail the body is,
And we are made
As only in decay
To lean and fade.
I think too much of death ;
There is a gloom
When I can't hear your breath
Calm in some room.

O, but how suddenly
Either may droop ;
Countenance be so white,
Body stoop.
Then there may be a place
Where fading flowers
Drop on a lifeless face
Through weeping hours.

Is then nothing safe ?
Can we not find
Some everlasting life
In our one mind ?
I feel it like disgrace
Only to understand
Your spirit through your word,
Or by your hand.

I cannot find a way
Through love and through ;
I cannot reach beyond
Body, to you.
When you or I must go
Down evermore,
There'll be no more to say
—But a locked door.

ALLOTMENTS

LIFTING through the broken clouds there shot
A searching beam of golden sunset-shine.
It swept the town allotments, plot by plot,
And all the digging clerks became divine—
Stood up like heroes with their spades of brass,
Turning the ore that made the realms of Spain !
So shone they for a moment. Then, alas !
The cloud-rift closed ; and they were clerks again.

MIRAGE

I SAW a man on a horse
Riding against the sun.
" Hallo ! Don Cossack ! " I cried.
He shouted, " Hallo, my son ! "

The Caspian Sea shimmered ;
The Kazak tents shone
For a moment in England,
Then the horseman was gone.

THE TRYST

THE mist is on the meadows,
Breast-high in the moon ;
And woodsmoke rises silver
O'er cold roofs of the town.

Now is the hour we longed for,
The solitude we planned.
But oh, this frozen passion
Was not by us designed !

N

DREAMS OF THE SEA

W. H. Davies

I KNOW not why I yearn for thee again,
  To sail once more upon thy fickle flood ;
I'll hear thy waves wash under my death-bed,
  Thy salt is lodged for ever in my blood.

Yet I have seen thee lash the vessel's sides
  In fury, with thy many-tailed whip ;
And I have seen thee, too, like Galilee,
  When Jesus walked in peace to Simon's ship.

And I have seen thy gentle breeze as soft
  As summer's, when it makes the cornfields run ;
And I have seen thy rude and lusty gale
  Make ships show half their bellies to the sun.

Thou knowest the way to tame the wildest life,
  Thou knowest the way to bend the great and proud :
I think of that Armada whose puffed sails,
  Greedy and large, came swallowing every cloud.

But I have seen the sea-boy, young and drowned,
  Lying on shore and, by thy cruel hand,
A seaweed beard was on his tender chin,
  His heaven-blue eyes were filled with common sand.

And yet, for all, I yearn for thee again,
  To sail once more upon thy fickle flood ;
I'll hear thy waves wash under my death-bed,
  Thy salt is lodged for ever in my blood.

QUEEN DJENIRA *Walter de la Mare*

WHEN Queen Djenira slumbers through
  The sultry noon's repose,
From out her dreams, as soft she lies,
  A faint thin music flows.

Her lovely hands lie narrow and pale
  With gilded nails, her head
Couched in its banded nets of gold
  Lies pillowed on her bed.

The little Nubian boys who fan
  Her cheeks and tresses clear,
Wonderful, wonderful, wonderful voices
  Seem afar to hear.

They slide their eyes, and nodding, say,
  ' Queen Djenira walks to-day
The courts of the lord Pthamasar
  Where the sweet birds of Psuthys are.'

And those of earth about her porch
  Of shadow cool and grey
Their sidelong beaks in silence lean,
  And silent flit away.

WHISPERS OF IMMORTALITY *T. S. Eliot*

WEBSTER was much possessed by death
And saw the skull beneath the skin ;
And breastless creatures under ground
Leaned backward with a lipless grin.

195

Daffodil bulbs instead of balls
Stared from the sockets of the eyes !
He knew that thought clings round dead limbs
Tightening its lusts and luxuries.

Donne, I suppose, was such another
Who found no substitute for sense ;
To seize and clutch and penetrate,
Expert beyond experience,

He knew the anguish of the marrow
The ague of the skeleton ;
No contact possible to flesh
Allayed the fever of the bone.

    .   .   .   .   .

Grishkin is nice : her Russian eye
Is underlined for emphasis ;
Uncorseted, her friendly bust
Gives promise of pneumatic bliss.

The couched Brazilian jaguar
Compels the scampering marmoset
With subtle effluence of cat ;
Grishkin has a maisonette ;

The sleek Brazilian jaguar
Does not in its arboreal gloom
Distil so rank a feline smell
As Grishkin in a drawing-room.

And even the Abstract Entities
Circumambulate her charm ;
But our lot crawls between dry ribs
To keep our metaphysics warm.

SNORE in the foam : the night is vast and blind,
The blanket of the mist around your shoulders,
Sleep your old sleep of rock, snore in the wind,
Snore in the spray !   The storm your slumber lulls,
His wings are folded on your nest of boulders
As on their eggs the grey wings of your gulls.

No more as when, ten thousand years ago,
You hissed a giant cinder from the ocean—
Around your rocks you furl the shawling snow,
Half sunk in your own darkness, vast and grim,
And round you on the deep with surly motion
Pivot your league-long shadow as you swim.

Why should you haunt me thus but that I know
My surly heart is in your own displayed,
Round whom such wastes in endless circuit flow,
Whose hours in such a gloomy compass run—
A dial with its league-long arm of shade
Slowly revolving to the moon and sun.

My heart has sunk, like your grey fissured crags,
By its own strength o'ertoppled and betrayed :
I too have burned the wind with fiery flags,
Who now am but a roost for empty words—
An island of the sea whose only trade
Is in the voyages of its wandering birds.

Did you not, when your strength became your pyre,
Deposed and tumbled from your flaming tower,
Awake in gloom from whence you sank in fire
To find Antaeus-like, more vastly grown,
A throne in your own darkness, and a power
Sheathed in the very coldness of your stone ?

Your strength is that you have no hope or fear,
You march before the world without a crown ;
The nations call you back, you do not hear :
The cities of the earth grow grey behind you,
You will be there when their great flames go down
And still the morning in the van will find you.

You march before the continents : you scout
In front of all the earth : alone you scale
The masthead of the world, a lorn look-out,
Waving the snowy flutter of your spray
And gazing back in infinite farewell
To suns that sink, and shores that fade away.

From your grey tower what long regrets you fling
To where, along the low horizon burning,
The great swan-breasted seraphs soar and sing,
And suns go down, and trailing splendours dwindle,
And sails on lonely errands unreturning,
Glow with a gold no sunrise can rekindle.

Turn to the Night, these flames are not for you
Whose steeple for the thunder swings its bells ;
Grey Memnon, to the tempest only true,
Turn to the night, turn to the shadowing foam,
And let your voice, the saddest of farewells,
With sullen curfew toll the grey wings home.

The wind your mournful syren haunts the gloom :
The rocks, spray-clouded, are your signal-guns
Whose stony nitre, puffed with flying spume,
Rolls forth in grim salute your broadside hollow,
Over the gorgeous burials of suns,
To sound the tocsin of the storms that follow.

Plunge forward ; like a ship to battle hurled,
Slip the long cables of the failing light,
The level rays that moor you to the world :
Sheathed in your armour of eternal frost,
Plunge forward, in the thunder of the fight
To lose yourself as I would fain be lost.

Exiled, like you, and severed from my race
By the cold ocean of my own disdain,
Do I not freeze in such a wintry space,
Do I not travel through a storm as vast
And rise at times, victorious from the main,
To fly the sunrise at my shattered mast ?

Your path is but a desert where you reap
Only the bitter knowledge of your soul,
You fish with nets of seaweed in the deep
As fruitlessly as I with nets of rhyme,
Yet forth you stride : yourself the way, the goal,
The surges are your strides, your path is time.

Hurled by what aim to what tremendous range !
A missile from the great sling of the past
Your passage leaves its track of death and change
And ruin on the world : you fly beyond,
Leaping the current of the ages vast
As lightly as a pebble skims a pond.

The years are undulations in your flight
Whose awful motion we can only guess :
Too swift for sense, too terrible for sight,
We only know how fast behind you darken
Our days like lonely beacons of distress :
We know that you stride on and will not harken.

Now in the eastern sky the fairest planet
Pierces the dying wave with dangled spear,
And in the whirring hollows of your granite
That vaster Sea, to which you are a shell,
Sighs with a ghostly rumour like the drear
Moan of the nightwind in a hollow cell.

We shall not meet again : over the wave
Our ways divide, and yours is straight and endless—
But mine is short and crooked to the grave :
Yet what of these dark crowds, amid whose flow
I battle like a rock, aloof and friendless—
Are not their generations, vague and endless,
The waves, the strides, the feet on which I go ?

"WHEN THE WORLD WAS IN BUILDING . . ."
Ford Madox Hueffer

THANK Goodness, the moving is over,
They've swept up the straw in the passage
And life will begin. . . .
This tiny, white, tiled cottage by the bridge ! . . .
When we've had tea I will punt you
To Paradise for the sugar and onions. . . .
We will drift home in the twilight,
The trout will be rising. . . .

"WHEN THE WORLD CRUMBLED"

ONCE there were purple seas—
Wide, wide. . . .
And myrtle-groves and cyclamen,
Above the cliff and the stone pines
Where a god watched. . . .

And thou, oh Lesbian . . .

Well, *that's* all done !

THREE Summers since I chose a maid,
  Too young maybe—but more's to do
At harvest-time than bide and woo.
  When us was wed she turned afraid
Of love and me and all things human ;
Like the shut of a winter's day.
Her smile went out, and 'twasn't a woman—
  More like a little frightened fay.
    One night, in the Fall, she runned away.

" Out 'mong the sheep, her be," they said,
'Should properly have been abed ;
But sure enough she wasn't there
Lying awake with her wide brown stare.
So over seven-acre field and up-along across the down
  We chased her, flying like a hare
Before our lanterns. To Church-Town
  All in a shiver and a scare
We caught her, fetched her home at last
  And turned the key upon her, fast.

She does the work about the house
As well as most, but like a mouse :
  Happy enough to chat and play
  With birds and rabbits and such as they,
  So long as men-folk keep away.
" Not near, not near ! " her eyes beseech
When one of us comes within reach.
  The women say that beasts in stall
  Look round like children at her call.
  I've hardly heard her speak at all.

Shy as a leveret, swift as he,
Straight and slight as a young larch tree,
Sweet as the first wild violets, she,
To her wild self. But what to me ?
The short days shorten and the oaks are brown,
    The blue smoke rises to the low grey sky,
One leaf in the still air falls slowly down,
    A magpie's spotted feathers lie
On the black earth spread white with rime,
The berries redden up to Christmas-time.
    What's Christmas-time without there be
    Some other in the house than we !

    She sleeps up in the attic there
        Alone, poor maid. 'Tis but a stair
    Betwixt us. Oh ! my God ! the down,
        The soft young down of her, the brown,
    The brown of her—her eyes, her hair, her hair !

JAM HIEMS TRANSIIT
Helen Parry Eden

WHEN the wind blows without the garden walls
Where from high vantage of the budding boughs
The wanton starling claps his wing and brawls
And finches to their half-erected house
Trail silver straws ; when on the sand-pit verges
The young lambs leap, when clouds on sunny tiles
Pass and re-pass, then the young Spring emerges
From Winter's fingers panoplied with smiles.
So some bright demoiselle but late returning
To her old home with new-acquirèd graces
Learnt in some strait academy and burning
To kindle wonderment in homely faces
Smileth, while she who taught her all her arts,
The dark duenna, with a sigh departs.

202

THE NEW HOUSE
Edward Thomas

Now first, as I shut the door,
    I was alone
In the new house ; and the wind
    Began to moan.

Old at once was the house,
    And I was old ;
My ears were teased with the dread
    Of what was foretold,

Nights of storm, days of mist, without end ;
    Sad days when the sun
Shone in vain : old griefs and griefs
    Not yet begun.

All was foretold me ; naught
    Could I foresee ;
But I learned how the wind would sound
    After these things should be.

THE LAW THE LAWYERS KNOW ABOUT
H. D. C. Pepler

THE law the lawyers know about
    Is property and land ;
But why the leaves are on the trees,
And why the waves disturb the seas,
Why honey is the food of bees,
Why horses have such tender knees,
Why winters come when rivers freeze,
Why Faith is more than what one sees,
And Hope survives the worst disease,
And Charity is more than these,
    They do not understand.

A DREAM IN EARLY SPRING　　*Fredegond Shove*

Now when I sleep the thrush breaks through my
　　dreams
With sharp reminders of the coming day :
After his call, one minute I remain
Unwaked, and on the darkness which is Me
There springs the image of a daffodil,
Growing upon a grassy bank alone,
And seeming with great joy his bell to fill
With drops of golden dew, which on the lawn
He shakes again, where they lie bright and chill.

His head is drooped ; the shrouded winds that sing
Bend him which way they will : never on earth
Was there before so beautiful a ghost ;
Alas, he had a less than flower-birth,
And like a ghost indeed must shortly glide
From all but the sad cells of memory,
Where he will linger, an imprisoned beam,
Or fallen shadow of the golden world,
Long after this and many another dream.

VARIATION ON A THEME BY ALEXANDER POPE
Sacheverell Sitwell

Now all the branches lift their arms
And the great Sun pours down his balms,
The leaves bud out, and wink their eyes
Gently lest a frost surprise.

Full is each river to the brim
Running so fast, its glass is dim,
Those rocks that burn in summer sun
Bow down to let the waters run.

All snows are melted from the hills
And fledgling birds now try their bills,
Or preen themselves in leaves' soft shade,
Dreaming of the flights they've made.

The gardener, stumbling, heavy shod,
Prints dew as though a bird had trod
By boughs that only want green sails
To start off down the panting gales.

Now do the Indian birds appear,
False summer, for they fly in fear
Floating to this cooler clime
Where through the leaves they sound their chime.

Far down in the myrtle grove
Wander the youths who died of love ;
And the hero's arméd shade
Glitters down the gloomy glade.

PENUMBRA   *Herbert Read*

IN this teashop
they seem so violent.
Why should they come here
dressed for tragedy ?

Did they anticipate
this genteel atmosphere ?
Her eyes are like moth-wings
furtive under a black arch.

She drinks a cup of tea.
But he is embarrassed—
stretches his gross neck
out of the white grip of his collar.

Sits uneasily
eagerly rises now she has done.
Anxiously seeks the looking-glass
then seeks the door.

She is gone
a vestal her robes fluttering
like a printed sheet
in the gusty Tube.

PRELUDE   *Richard Aldington*

How could I love you more ?
I would give up
Even that beauty I have loved too well
That I might love you better.
Alas, how poor the gifts that lovers give—
I can but give you of my flesh and strength,
I can but give you these few passing days
And passionate words that since our speech began
All lovers whisper in all women's ears.

I try to think of some one gift
No lover yet in all the world has found ;
I think : If the cold sombre gods
Were hot with love as I am
Could they not endow you with a star
And fix bright youth for ever in your limbs ?
Could they not give you all things that I lack ?

You should have loved a god ; I am but dust.
Yet no god loved as loves this poor frail dust.

AN INTERLUDE

THERE is a momentary pause in love
When all the birth-pangs of desire are lulled . . .

I wait,
And glide upon the crested surge of days
Like some sea-god, with tangled, dripping beard
And smooth hard skin, who glimpses from the sea
An earth-girl naked by the long foam fringe,
And, utterly forgetting all his life,
Hurries toward her, glad with sudden love.

Even in that pause of speed I live ;
And though the great wave curl in spikes of foam
And crash me bleeding at her cool small feet
All breathless with the water's sudden swirl,
I shall be glad of every stabbing wound
If she will hold my tired limbs to hers
And breathe wild love into my mouth and thrill
Even the blood I shed with that desire
Which throbs all through me at her lightest touch.

EPILOGUE

HAVE I spoken too much or not enough of love ?
Who can tell ?

But we who do not drug ourselves with lies
Know, with how deep a pathos, that we have
Only the warmth and beauty of this life
Before the blankness of the unending gloom.
Here for a little while we see the sun
And smell the grape-vines on the terraced hills,
And sing and weep, fight, starve and feast, and love
Lips and soft breasts too sweet for innocence.

And in this little glow of mortal life—
Faint as one candle in a large cold room—
We know the clearest light is shed by love,
That when we kiss with life-blood in our lips,
Then we are nearest to the dreamed-of gods.

WINTER THE HUNTSMAN

Osbert Sitwell

THROUGH his iron glades
Rides Winter the Huntsman.
All colour fades
As his horn is heard sighing.

Far through the forest
His wild hooves crash and thunder
Till many a mighty branch
Is torn asunder.

And the red reynard creeps
To his hole near the river,
The copper leaves fall
And the bare trees shiver,

As night creeps from the ground,
Hides each tree from its brother,
And each dying sound
Reveals yet another.

Is it Winter the Huntsman
Who gallops through his iron glades,
Cracking his cruel whip
To the gathering shades?

THE MAIN-DEEP

James Stephens

THE long-rólling,
Steady-póuring,
Deep-trenchéd
Green billów:

The wide-topped,
Unbróken,
Green-glacid,
Slow-sliding,

Cold-flushing,
—On—on—on—
Chill-rushing,
Hush—hushing,

. . . Hush—hushing . . .

THE LAMP IN THE EMPTY ROOM

Humbert Wolfe

I LOOKED back suddenly into the empty room,
and saw the lamp that I had lit
still shining on the little table by the window,
and throwing its light on the tumbled sheets of paper
on which I had been writing.
And I felt as though long years ago
a man, whom I had known very little,
had lighted that lamp, and sat by the window
writing and believing that he was a poet,
and then he came out of the room and found the letter . . .
He will not go into the room again :
and not he, but I will go in softly
and put out the lamp, and lay aside
the useless paper.

THE SHEETED LIVING

LEAVE the dead to bury their dead !
    I'll keep my grieving
for the cold, unburiéd,
    but sheeted living.

O

Ghosts they wander by street and mart,
   and that one says to this one :
" O had I never had a heart
   I should not now so miss one."

But this one says " O brother, brother,
   when once your heart is lost,
at least you cannot break another,
   and that is something, ghost."

OREAD

H. D.

Whirl up, sea—
Whirl your pointed pines,
Splash your great pines
On our rocks,
Hurl your green over us,
Cover us with your pools of fir.

SEA ROSE

Rose, harsh rose,
marred and with stint of petals,
meagre flower, thin,
sparse of leaf,

more precious
than a wet rose
single on a stem—
you are caught in the drift.

Stunted, with small leaf,
you are flung on the sand,
you are lifted
in the crisp sand
that drives in the wind.

Can the spice-rose
drip such acrid fragrance
hardened in a leaf ?

METAMORPHOSIS (Extract) *Edith Sitwell*

*   *   *

How terrible these winter nights must be
To the deserted Dead . . . if we could see

The eternal anguish of the skeleton,
So fleshless even the dog leaves it alone,

Atridæ-like devouring its own blood
With hopeless love beneath the earth's blind hood :
For warmth, the rags of flesh about the bone
Devoured by black disastrous dreams, alone

The worm is their companion, vast years
Pile mountain-high above, and the last tears

Freeze to gigantic polar nights of ice
Around the heart through crumbling centuries.

O Dead, your heart is gone, it cannot weep !
From decency the skeleton must sleep.

O heart, shrink out of sight, you have no flesh
For love or dog or worm to court afresh,

Only your youthful smile is mirrored lone
In that eternity the skeleton.

For never come they now, nor comes the hour
When your lips spoke, and winter broke in flower,

The Parthenon was built by your dead kiss.
What should they seek, now you are changed to this

Vast craggy bulk, strong as the prophet's rock ?
No grief tears waters from that stone to mock
Death's immobility, and changed to stone
Those eyelids see one sight and one alone.

What do they see ?   Some lost and childish kiss
In summers ere they knew that love was this,

The terrible Gehenna of the bone
Deserted by the flesh, tears changed to stone ?

Or do they blame us that we walk this earth,
Who are more dead than they, nor seek rebirth

Nor change ?   The snowflake's six-rayed star can see
Rock-crystal's cold six-rayed eternity,—

Thus light grief melts in craggy waterfalls ;
But mine melts never, though the last spring calls ;

The polar night's huge boulder hath rolled this
My heart, my Sisyphus, in the abyss.

Do the Dead know the nights wherein we grope
From our more terrible abyss of hope
To soft despair ?   The nights when creeping Fear
Crumples our hearts, knowing when age appear

Our sun, our love, will leave us more alone
Than the black mouldering rags about the bone ?

Age shrinks our hearts to ape-like dust . . . that ape
Looks through the eyes where all death's chasms gape

Between ourself and what we used to be.
My soul, my Lazarus, know you not me ?

Am I so changed by Time's appalling night ?
'Tis but my bone that cannot stand upright,

That leans as if it thirsted . . . for what spring ?
The ape's bent skeleton foreshadowing,

With head bent from the light, its only kiss.
Do the Dead know that metamorphosis

When the appalling lion-claws of age
With talons tear the cheek and heart, yet rage

For life devours the bone, a tigerish fire ?
But quenched in the vast empire of the mire

These craters cry not to the eternal bone :
The Dead may hide the changing skeleton.

So quench the light, my Lazarus, nor see
The thing we are, the thing that we might be :

In mouldering cerements of that thick grave
Our flesh, we lose the one light that could save.

But yet it shall avail that grass shall sing
From loveless bones in some foreshadowed spring,

And summer break from a long-shadowed kiss
Though our dry bones are sunless grown as this,

And eyeless statues, broken and alone
In shadeless avenues, the music gone,
We stand . . . the leaves we knew are black as jet
Though the light scatters feathers on them yet,

Remembering sylvan nymphs. . . .

HORSES

Edwin Muir

THOSE lumbering horses in the steady plough,
On the bare field—I wonder why, just now,
They seemed so terrible, so wild and strange,
Like magic power on the stony grange.

Perhaps some childish hour has come again,
When I watched fearful, through the blackening rain,
Their hooves like pistons in an ancient mill
Move up and down, yet seem as standing still.

Their conquering hooves which trod the stubble down
Were ritual which turned the field to brown,
And their great hulks were seraphim of gold,
Or mute ecstatic monsters on the mould.

And oh the rapture, when, one furrow done,
They marched broad-breasted to the sinking sun !
The light flowed off their bossy sides in flakes ;
The furrows rolled behind like struggling snakes.

But when at dusk with steaming nostrils home
They came, they seemed gigantic in the gloam,
And warm and glowing with mysterious fire,
Which lit their smouldering bodies in the mire.

Their eyes as brilliant and as wide as night
Gleamed with a cruel apocalyptic sight.
Their manes the leaping ire of the wind
Lifted with rage invisible and blind.

Ah now it fades ! it fades ! and I must pine
Again for that dread country crystalline,
Where the blank field and the still-standing tree
Were bright and fearful presences to me.

A PRAYER
James Joyce

AGAIN!
Come, give, yield all your strength to me!
From far a low word breathes on the breaking brain
Its cruel calm, submission's misery,
Gentling her awe as to a soul predestined.
Cease, silent love! My doom!

Blind me with your dark nearness, O have mercy, beloved
    enemy of my will!
I dare not withstand the cold touch that I dread.
Draw from me still
My slow life! Bend deeper on me, threatening head,
Proud by my downfall, remembering, pitying
Him who is, him who was!

Again!
Together, folded by the night, they lay on earth. I hear
From far her low word breathe on my breaking brain.
Come! I yield. Bend deeper upon me! I am here.
Subduer, do not leave me! Only joy, only anguish,
Take me, save me, soothe me, O spare me.

THE MUMMER
Anna Wickham

STRICT I walk my ordered way
Through the strait and duteous day;
The hours are nuns that summon me
To offices of huswifry.
Cups and cupboards, flagons, food
Are things of my solicitude.
No elfin Folly haply strays
Down my precise and well-swept ways.

215

When that compassionate lady Night
Shuts out a prison from my sight,
With other thrift I turn a key
Of the old chest of Memory.
And in my spacious dreams unfold
A flimsy stuff of green and gold,
And walk and wander in the dress
Of old delights, and tenderness.

TREES (EXTRACT) *Harold Monro*

THERE are some men, of course, some men, I know,
Who, when they pass,
Seem like trees walking, and to grow
From earth, and, native in the grass,
(So taut their muscles) move on gliding roots.
They blossom every day : their fruits
Are always new and cover the happy ground,
Wherever they may stand
You hear inevitable sound
Of birds and branches, harvest and all delights
Of pastured and wooded land.
For them it is not dangerous to go
Each side that barrier moving to and fro :
They without trepidation undertake
Excursions into sleep, and safely come awake.

But it is different, different for me,
(Also for you I fear)
To whom a tree seems something more than tree,
And when we see,
Clustered together, two or three,
We almost are afraid to pass them near.
How beautifully they grow,
Above their stiles and lanes and watery places,
Crowding the brink of silence everywhere,

With branches dipping low
To smile toward us or to stroke our faces.
They drown us in their summer, and swirl round,
Leaving us faint : so nobody is free,
But always some surrounding ground
Is swamped and washed and covered in by tree.

They follow us and haunt us. We must build
Houses of wood. Our evening rooms are filled
With fragments of the forest : chairs and tables.
We swing our wooden doors ;
Pile up, divide our sheds, byres, stables
With logs, make wooden stairs, lay wooden floors,
Sit, move, and sleep among the limbs of trees,
Rejoicing to be near them. How men saw,
Chisel and hammer, carve and tease
All timber to their purpose, modelling
The forest in their chambers. And the raw
Wild stuff, built like a cupboard or a shelf,
Will crack and shiver in the night, and sing,
Reminding everybody of itself ;
Out of decayed old centuries will bring
A sudden memory
Of growing tree.

SMALL BIRDS   *Peter Quennell*

SMALL birds who sweep into a tree
—A storm of fluttering, stilled as suddenly,
Making the light slip round a shaken berry,
Swinging slim sunlight twigs uncertainly,
Are moved by ripples of light discontent
—Quick waves of anger, breaking through the tree
Into a foam of riot—voices high
And tart as a sloe-berry.

OH ! Sorrow, Sorrow, scarce I knew
  Your name when, shaking down the may
In sport, a little child, I grew
  Afraid to find you at my play.
I heard it ere I looked at you ;
  You sang it softly as you came
Bringing your little boughs of yew
  To fling across my gayest game.

Oh ! Sorrow, Sorrow, was I fair
  That when I decked me for a bride,
You met me stepping down the stair
  And led me from my lover's side ?
Was I so dear you could not spare
  The maid to love, the child to play,
But coming always unaware,
  Must bid and beckon me away ?

Oh ! Sorrow, Sorrow, is my bed
  So wide and warm that you must lie
Upon it ; toss your weary head
  And stir my slumber with your sigh ?
I left my love at your behest,
  I waved your little boughs of yew,
But, Sorrow, Sorrow, let me rest,
  For oh ! I cannot sleep with you !

THE MAN WITH A HAMMER *Anna Wickham*

MY Dear was a mason
And I was his stone.
And quick did he fashion
A house of his own.

As fish in the waters,
As birds in a tree,
So natural and blithe lives
His spirit in me.

THE HEART'S JOURNEY (V)   *Siegfried Sassoon*

You were glad to-night; and now you've gone away.
Flushed in the dark you put your dreams to bed;
But as you fall asleep I hear you say
Those tired sweet drowsy words we left unsaid.

Sleep well: for I can follow you to bless
And lull your distant beauty where you roam;
And with wild songs of hoarded loveliness
Recall you to these arms that were your home.

THE HEART'S JOURNEY (XXXIV)

A FLOWER has opened in my heart . . .
What flower is this, what flower of spring,
What simple, secret thing?
It is the peace that shines apart,
The peace of daybreak skies that bring
Clear song and wild swift wing.

Heart's miracle of inward light,
What powers unknown have sown your seed
And your perfection freed? . . .
O flower within me wondrous white,
I know you only as my need
And my unsealed sight.

SEE, they return ; ah, see the tentative
Movements, and the slow feet,
The trouble in the pace and the uncertain
Wavering !

See, they return, one, and by one,
With fear, as half-awakened ;
As if the snow should hesitate
And murmur in the wind,
                and half turn back ;
These were the ' Wing'd-with-Awe,'
                Inviolable.

Gods of the winged shoe !
With them the silver hounds,
                sniffing the trace of air !

Haie ! Haie !
                These were the swift to harry ;
These the keen-scented ;
These were the souls of blood.

Slow on the leash,
                pallid the leash-men !

APPARUIT

GOLDEN rose the house, in the portal I saw
thee, a marvel, carven in subtle stuff, a
portent. Life died down in the lamp and
flickered,
                caught at the wonder.

Crimson, frosty with dew, the roses bend where
thou afar, moving in the glamorous sun,
drinkst in life of earth, of the air, the tissue
                golden about thee.

Green the ways, the breath of the fields is thine there,
open lies the land, yet the steely going
darkly hast thou dared and the dreaded æther
         parted before thee.

Swift at courage thou in the shell of gold, cast-
ing a-loose the cloak of the body, camest
straight then shone thine oriel and the stunned light
         faded about thee.

Half the graven shoulder, the throat aflash with
strands of light inwoven about it, loveliest of all things, frail alabaster, ah me !
         swift in departing.

Clothed in goldish weft, delicately perfect,
gone as wind ! The cloth of the magical hands !
Thou a slight thing, thou in access of cunning
         dar'dst to assume this ?

THE LOVER (1917)   *Richard Aldington*

         THOUGH I have had friends
         And a beautiful love
         There is one lover I await above all.

         She will not come to me
         In the time of soft plum-blossoms
         When the air is gay with birds singing
         And the sky is a delicate caress ;
         She will come
         From the midst of a vast clamour
         With a mist of stars about her
         And great beckoning plumes of smoke
         Upon her leaping horses.

                                        221

And she will bend suddenly and clasp me;
She will clutch me with fierce arms
And stab me with a kiss like a wound
That bleeds slowly.

But though she will hurt me at first
In her strong gladness
She will soon soothe me gently
And cast upon me an unbreakable sleep
Softly for ever.

SHE MOVED THROUGH THE FAIR

Padraic Colum

MY young love said to me, " My brothers won't mind,
And my parents won't slight you for your lack of kind."
Then she stepped away from me, and this she did say,
" It will not be long, love, till our wedding day."

She stepped away from me and she moved through the
    fair,
And fondly I watched her go here and go there,
Then she went her way homeward with one star awake,
As the swan in the evening moves over the lake.

The people were saying no two were e'er wed
But one had a sorrow that never was said,
And I smiled as she passed with her goods and her gear,
And that was the last that I saw of my dear.

I dreamt it last night that my young love came in,
So softly she entered, her feet made no din;
She came close beside me, and this she did say,
" It will not be long, love, till our wedding day."

JOURNEY'S END

Humbert Wolfe

WHAT will they give me, when journey's done ?
Your own room to be quiet in, Son !

Who shares it with me ? There is none
shares that cool dormitory, Son !

Who turns the sheets ? There is but one
And no one needs to turn it, Son.

Who lights the candle ? Everyone
sleeps without candle all night, Son.

Who calls me after sleeping ? Son,
You are not called when journey's done.

MUTATIONS OF THE PHŒNIX (VII)

Herbert Read

PHŒNIX, bird of terrible pride,
ruddy eye and iron beak !
Come, leave the incinerary nest ;
spread your red wings.

And soaring in the golden light
survey the world ;
hover against the highest sky ;
menace men with your strange phenomena.

For a haunt seek a coign
in a rocky land ;
when the night is black
settle on the bleak headlands.

Utter shrill warnings in the cold dawn sky ;
let them descend
into the shuttered minds below you.
Inhabit our withered nerves.

223

DAPHNE—AN ADAPTATION FROM JOHN MILTON

Sacheverell Sitwell

THAT day he met me in the field
I ran from him and would not yield ;
Where he holds me with strong arm
There my boughs send forth their balm ;

My locks, bright river in the sun,
Are golden leaves while we still run.

Nard and Cassia breathe through me
Since he cruelly chased and slew me ;
Embalming me in living death,
While I yet fired him with my breath.

Now as a tree, I'm safe at last,
And, though he runs, I need not haste.

Every day he walks this wood
And swiftly comes to where we stood ;
Each morning I'm a tree again,
Blown sweeter by his tears, the rain ;

His hot hands comb my hair once more,
Yellow as amber on the shore.

He leaves me, thinking I am dead
While my sweet breathing fans his head ;
The winds, my breath, will follow him
Until he cools, and day grows dim ;

Nard and Cassia's balmy smells
Fill the chambers where he dwells.

THE TOWER

Robert Nichols

It was deep night, and over Jerusalem's low roofs
The moon floated, drifting through high vaporous woofs.
The moonlight crept and glistened silent, solemn, sweet,
Over dome and column, up empty, endless street ;
In the closed, scented gardens the rose loosed from the
　　stem
Her white showery petals ;　none regarded them ;
The starry thicket breathed odours to the sentinel palm ;
Silence possessed the city like a soul possessed by calm.

Not a spark in the warren under the giant night,
Save where in a turret's lantern beamed a grave, still light :
There in the topmost chamber a gold-eyed lamp was lit—
Marvellous lamp in darkness, informing, redeeming it !
For, set in that tiny chamber, Jesus, the blessed and
　　doomed,
Spoke to the lone apostles as light to men entombed ;
And spreading his hands in blessing, as one soon to be dead,
He put soft enchantment into spare wine and bread.

The hearts of the disciples were broken and full of tears,
Because their lord, the spearless, was hedged about with
　　spears ;
And in his face the sickness of departure had spread a gloom,
At leaving his young friends friendless.
　　　　　They could not forget the tomb.

He smiled subduedly, telling, in tones soft as voice of the
　　dove,
The endlessness of sorrow, the eternal solace of love ;
And lifting the earthly tokens, wine and sorrowful bread,
He bade them sup and remember one who lived and was
　　dead.
And they could not restrain their weeping.
　　　　　But one rose up to depart,

P

Having weakness and hate of weakness raging within his
  heart,
And bowed to the robed assembly whose eyes gleamed
  wet in the light.
Judas arose and departed : night went out to the night.

Then Jesus lifted his voice like a fountain in an ocean of
  tears,
And comforted his disciples and calmed and allayed
  their fears.
But Judas wound down the turret, creeping from floor to
  floor,
And would fly ; but one leaning, weeping, barred him
  beside the door.
And he knew her by her ruddy garment and two yet-
  watching men :
Mary of Seven Evils, Mary Magdalen.
And he was frighted at her. She sighed : ' I dreamed
  him dead.
We sell the body for silver . . . '
                Then Judas cried out and fled
Forth into the night ! . . .   The moon had begun to set :
A drear, deft wind went sifting, setting the dust afret ;
Into the heart of the city Judas ran on and prayed
To stern Jehovah lest his deed make him afraid.

But in the tiny lantern, hanging as if on air,
The disciples sat unspeaking. Amaze and peace were there.
For *his* voice, more lovely than song of all earthly birds,
In accents humble and happy spoke slow, consoling words.

Thus Jesus discoursed, and was silent, sitting upright,
  and soon
Past the casement behind him slanted the sinking moon ;
And, rising for Olivet, all stared, between love and dread,
Seeing the torrid moon a ruddy halo behind his head.

REMINISCENCE (V)   *Padraic Colum*

OVER old walls the Laburnums
    hang cones of fire ;
Laburnums that grow out of old
    mould in old gardens :

Old men and old maids who have money or pensions
Have shuttered themselves in the pales of old gardens.

The gardens grow wild ; out of their mould the
    Laburnums
Draw cones of fire.

And we, who've no lindens, no palms, no cedars of
    Lebanon,
Rejoice you have gardens with mould, old men and old
    maids :

The bare and the dusty streets have now the Laburnums,
Have now cones of fire !

MORNING AT THE WINDOW   *T. S. Eliot*

THEY are rattling breakfast plates in basement kitchens,
And along the trampled edges of the street
I am aware of the damp souls of housemaids
Sprouting despondently at area gates.

The brown waves of fog toss up to me
Twisted faces from the bottom of the street,
And tear from a passer-by with muddy skirts
An aimless smile that hovers in the air
And vanishes along the level of the roofs.

THEY say he stopped his horse and talked to her
Some minutes' length upon the mossy bridge.
But that I doubt, for she has never said,
Since she was ill and numbered with the dead,
Whether he spoke, or merely reined his horse,
And gazed in sorrow over the balustrade.
These emperors of men are not so free
As gossip presupposes them to be,
Of speech with common folk. They do not greet
Upon the road, but ride with fixed resolve
And that immortal patience of the great,
Which cloaks them round in sombre dreams of fate.
They are expectant people, waiting one
Who should arrive, to meet them on the way
With messages of some remote affray
Unheard of in the lands through which they pass.
He may have stopped. I cannot think he spoke.

THE SHIP

SWINGING round into harbour
Came the ship.
I saw it through her blown hair
As we stood lip to lip.

The ardour faded between us.
Cold and still,
We watched the ship drop anchor
In the shadow of the hill.

THE SCAPEGOAT
Sylvia Townsend Warner

SEE the scapegoat, happy beast,
From every personal sin released,
And in the desert hidden apart,
Dancing with a careless heart.

'Lightly weigh the sins of others.'
See him skip! 'Am I my brother's
Keeper? O never, no, no, no!
Lightly come and lightly go!'

In the town, from sin made free,
Righteous men hold jubilee.
In the desert all alone
The scapegoat dances on and on.

SONG FROM THE BRIDE OF SMITHFIELD

A THOUSAND guileless sheep have bled,
A thousand bullocks knelt in fear,
To daub my Henry's cheek with red
And round the curl above his ear.

And wounded calves hung up to drip
Have in slow sweats distilled for him
The dew that polishes his lip,
The inward balm that oils each limb.

In vain I spread my maiden arts,
In vain for Henry's love I pine.
He is too skilled in bleeding hearts
To turn this way and pity mine.

THE tree has entered my hands,
The sap has ascended my arms,
The tree has grown in my breast—
Downward,
The branches grow out of me, like arms.

Trees you are,
Moss you are,
You are violets with wind above them.
A child—*so* high—you are,
And all this is folly to the world.

THE EYES

REST Master, for we be a-weary, weary
And would feel the fingers of the wind
Upon these lids that lie over us
Sodden and lead-heavy.

Rest brother, for lo ! the dawn is without !
The yellow flame paleth
And the wax runs low.

Free us, for without be goodly colours,
Green of the wood-moss and flower colours,
And coolness beneath the trees.

Free us, for we perish
In this ever-flowing monotony
Of ugly print marks, black
Upon white parchment.

Free us, for there is one
Whose smile more availeth
Than all the age-old knowledge of thy books :
And we would look thereon.

THE SONG OF THE MAD PRINCE

Walter de la Mare

WHO said, ' Peacock Pie ' ?
  The old King to the sparrow :
Who said, ' Crops are ripe ' ?
  Rust to the harrow :
Who said, ' Where sleeps she now ?
  Where rests she now her head,
Bathed in eve's loveliness ' ?—
  That's what I said.

Who said, ' Ay, mum's the word ' ?
  Sexton to willow :
Who said, ' Green dusk for dreams,
  Moss for a pillow ' ?
Who said, ' All Time's delight
  Hath she for narrow bed ;
Life's troubled bubble broken ' ?—
  That's what I said.

REFLECTION

W. J. Turner

' IT is a symbol of the life we have known '—
Thus he spake, lifting eyes from the book
Into the calm afternoon
Where the trees played their silver-fretted tune
Netting the wind
On the sky's beach smooth as stone.

In the imagination alone
Love, entwined in a look,
Drinks without trembling of lip
Itself in a *Shape* unknown—
As the wind drunken in a ship
Rolls on the sea calm-blown.

231

But fishermen whom the wind forsook
Marooned on the margin stand,
Not the waving of a hand
Nor soundless flight of a look
Parts the tumbling sailors who drowned
From their images upright on land.

What falling through fathoms of glass
Erect on the sea-shore stands
Shading eyes with hands
Is that image shut-off, alone,
Victim of imaginary mass
Shadow of the reader in the book.

Something of the sky has flown
Into the wings of the dove ;
Darkening the day's still grove
The *shadow* of the reader has gone
Into the hollow of love—
Hysteria calmed into stone.

In imagination no longer entwined
They whom perfection forsook
Shattered the ideal in the mind ;
Passionlessly lip fell from lip
As wind falls in billow behind
The onward—vanishing ship.

A breeze has broken the glass,
The silver fleece on the sand—
Sign wherever Jason shall pass
Of virginity raped from the land
By Venuses soft gold hand—
For of *Argos* the story was.

UNDER

J. C. Squire

IN this house, she said, in this high second storey,
In this room where we sit, over the midnight street,
There runs a rivulet, narrow but very rapid,
Under the still floor and your unconscious feet.

The lamp on the table made a cone of light
That spread to the base of the walls : above was in
  gloom.
I heard her words with surprise ; had I worked here so
  long,
And never divined that secret of the room ?

" But how," I asked, " does the water climb so high ? "
" I do not know," she said, " but the thing is there ;
Pull up the boards while I go and fetch you a rod."
She passed, and I heard her creaking descend the stair.

And I rose and rolled the Turkey carpet back
From the two broad boards by the north wall she had
  named,
And, hearing already the crumple of water, I knelt
And lifted the first of them up ; and the water gleamed,

Bordered with little frosted heaps of ice,
And, as she came back with a rod and line that swung,
I moved the other board ; in the yellow light
The water trickled frostily, slackly along.

I took the tackle, a stiff black rubber worm,
That stuck out its pointed tail from a cumbrous hook.
" But there can't be fishing in water like this," I said,
And she, with weariness, " There is no ice there. Look."

233

And I stood there, gazing down at a stream in spate,
Holding the rod in my undecided hand . . .
Till it all in a moment grew smooth and still and clear,
And along its deep bottom of slaty grey sand

Three scattered little trout, as black as tadpoles,
Came waggling slowly along the glass-dark lake,
And I swung my arm to drop my pointing worm in,
And then I stopped again with a little shake.

For I heard the thin gnat-like voices of the trout
—My body felt woolly and sick and astray and cold—
Crying with mockery in them : " You are not allowed
To take us, you know, under ten years old."

And the room swam, the calm woman and the yellow
    lamp,
The table, and the dim-glistering walls, and the floor,
And the stream sank away, and all whirled dizzily,
And I moaned, and the pain at my heart grew more and
    more,

And I fainted away, utterly miserable,
Falling in a place where there was nothing to pass,
Knowing all sorrows and the mothers and sisters of
    sorrows,
And the pain of the darkness before anything ever was.

HUNGER
Laurence Binyon

I COME among the peoples like a shadow.
I sit down by each man's side.

None sees me, but they look on one another,
And know that I am there.

My silence is like the silence of the tide
That buries the playground of children ;

Like the deepening of frost in the slow night,
When birds are dead in the morning.

Armies trample, invade, destroy,
With guns roaring from earth and air.

I am more terrible than armies,
I am more feared than the cannon.

Kings and chancellors give commands ;
I give no command to any ;

But I am listened to more than kings
And more than passionate orators.

I unswear words, and undo deeds.
Naked things know me.

I am first and last to be felt of the living.
I am Hunger.

GALLIPOLI (ANNIVERSARY)   *Mary Morison Webster*

GHOSTS man the phantom ships that ply between.
White ships with sails of mist and bleaching prows,
Ply through the night, with freight of unkept vows
And haggard men. The waters stretching green
Into the distant bay, roll to the shore
With ominous music, and the dawn creeps slow
On frightened feet across the hills, till lo,
The ghastly prows are turned, and there once more
The boats are lowered and filled, and through the dark
Bewildered waters crouching men cling close
On anxious oars. " A landing ! Now ! " Dim rows
Bleeding, insensate, mark the waiting sand,
Heedless they rush, blanched, frenzied, staring, stark,
Dead man,—eternally, they land, they land !

THE GARDENER   *Sacheverell Sitwell*

STAND still, sun, let the summer day burn slow,
For I must snare the gardener with a stretch of notes,
Catch him alive with words as in a web.
O, brittle cage to hold back such a throat of fire !
I build the bars now for his wings to beat on ;
See, I hold him prisoner !
His wide hat cooler than a whole tree's shade
Like the snow cap on a mountain shelters him :
As he bows among the flower-beds in the beating sun
The leaves are fanning him
Like the cool flow of stars above the hot sun's face,
Dancing trees for running water.
Mute as me for speech,
And yet his throat were like a nightingale's
Had he but power to sing :
Like a boat's neck on the water should he ride in air
On those slow tides, the summer winds—

He shall float among the boughs where birds are singing
As light as wind who sighs in the cornfield
And, at night, lies hid in leaves :
Till those plumes come,
He will pace his Kingdom by loud starlight
On tiptoe past the windows
Listening to the harp's loud beat,
In case a sash should open while music masks the noise,
And Cherubino, like a flash of stars, be gone again.

CHAMBER MUSIC (XXXVI) *James Joyce*

I HEAR an army charging upon the land
    And the thunder of horses plunging, foam about their
      knees.
Arrogant, in black armour, behind them stand,
    Disdaining the reins, with fluttering whips, the
      charioteers.

They cry unto the night their battlename :
    I moan in sleep when I hear afar their whirling laughter.
They cleave the gloom of dreams, a blinding flame,
    Clanging, clanging upon the heart as upon an anvil.

They come shaking in triumph their long green hair :
    They come out of the sea and run shouting by the
      shore.
My heart, have you no wisdom thus to despair ?
    My love, my love, my love, why have you left me
      alone ?

STREET-WALKERS *D. H. Lawrence*

WHEN into the night the yellow light is roused like dust
    above the towns,
Or like a mist the moon has kissed from off a pool in the
    midst of the downs,

Our faces flower for a little hour pale and uncertain along
    the street,
Daisies that waken all mistaken white-spread in expect-
    ancy to meet

The luminous mist which the poor things wist was dawn
    arriving across the sky,
When dawn is far behind the star the dust-lit town has
    driven so high.

All the birds are folded in a silent ball of sleep,
    All the flowers are faded from the asphalt isle in the
        sea,
Only we hard-faced creatures go round and round, and
    keep
The shores of this innermost ocean alive and illusory.

Wanton sparrows that twittered when morning looked in
    at their eyes
    And the Cyprian's pavement-roses are gone, and now
        it is we
Flowers of illusion who shine in our gauds, make a Para-
    dise
On the shores of this ceaseless ocean, gay birds of the
    town-dark sea.

FUTILITY

Wilfred Owen

MOVE him into the sun—
Gently its touch awoke him once,
At home, whispering of fields unsown.
Always it woke him, even in France,
Until this morning and this snow.
If anything might rouse him now
The kind old sun will know.

Think how it wakes the seeds—
Woke, once, the clays of a cold star.
Are limbs so dear-achieved, are sides
Full-nerved,—still warm,—too hard to stir ?
Was it for this the clay grew tall ?
—O what made fatuous sunbeams toil
To break earth's sleep at all ?

JOURNEY OF THE MAGI

T. S. Eliot

' A COLD coming we had of it,
Just the worst time of the year
For a journey, and such a long journey :
The ways deep and the weather sharp,
The very dead of winter.'
And the camels galled, sore-footed, refractory,
Lying down in the melting snow.
There were times we regretted
The summer palaces on slopes, the terraces,
And the silken girls bringing sherbet.
Then the camel men cursing and grumbling
And running away, and wanting their liquor and women,
And the night-fires going out, and the lack of shelters,
And the cities hostile and the towns unfriendly
And the villages dirty and charging high prices :
A hard time we had of it.

At the end we preferred to travel all night,
Sleeping in snatches,
With the voices singing in our ears, saying
That this was all folly.
Then at dawn we came down to a temperate valley,
Wet, below the snow line, smelling of vegetation ;
With a running stream and a water-mill beating the dark-
    ness,
And three trees on the low sky,
And an old white horse galloped away in the meadow.
Then we came to a tavern with vine-leaves over the lintel,
Six hands at an open door dicing for pieces of silver,
And feet kicking the empty wine-skins.
But there was no information, and so we continued
And arrived at evening, not a moment too soon
Finding the place ; it was (you may say) satisfactory.

All this was a long time ago, I remember,
And I would do it again, but set down
This set down
This : were we led all that way for
Birth or Death ? There was a Birth, certainly,
We had evidence and no doubt. I had seen birth and
    death,
But had thought they were different ; this Birth was
Hard and bitter agony for us, like Death, our death.
We returned to our places, these Kingdoms,
But no longer at ease here, in the old dispensation,
With an alien people clutching their gods.
I should be glad of another death.

No more upon my bosom rest thee,
Too often have my hands caressed thee,
   My lips thou knowest well, too well.
Lean to my heart no more thine ear
My spirit's hidden truth to hear
   —It has no more to tell.

In what dark night, in what strange night,
Burnt to the butt the candle's light
   That lit our room so long ?
I do not know. I thought I knew
How love could be both sweet and true,
   I also thought it strong.

Where has the flame departed, where
Amid the waste of empty air
   Is that which dwelt with us ?
Was it a fancy ? Did we make
Only a show for dead love's sake,
   It being so piteous ?

No more against my bosom press thee,
Ask no more that my hands caress thee,
   Leave the sad lips thou hast known so well.
If to my heart thou lean thine ear,
There, grieving, thou wilt only hear
   Vain murmuring of an empty shell.

WHEN ALL IS SAID

J. D. C. Pellow

WHEN all is said
And all is done
Beneath the Sun,
And Man lies dead ;

When all the earth
Is a cold grave,
And no more brave
Bright things have birth

When cooling sun
And stone-cold world,
Together hurled,
Flame up as one—

O Sons of Men,
When all is flame,
What of your fame
And splendour then ?

When all is fire
And flaming air,
What of your rare
And high desire

To turn the clod
To a thing divine,
The earth a shrine,
And Man the God ?

INDEX OF AUTHORS

244

INDEX OF TITLES

251

Printed in **Great Britain** by Butler & Tanner Ltd., Frome and London